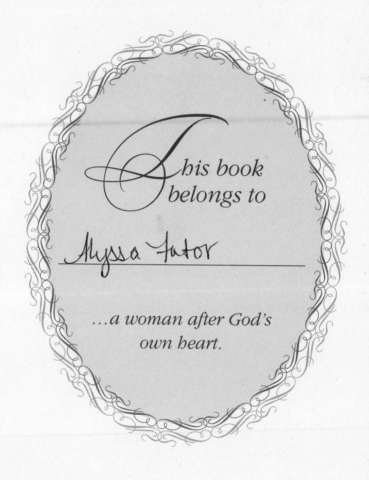

*T*his book
belongs to

Alyssa Tator

*...a woman after God's
own heart.*

Becoming a Woman of Beauty & Strength

Elizabeth George

HARVEST HOUSE PUBLISHERS
Eugene, Oregon 97402

Cover by Terry Dugan Design, Bloomington, Minnesota

Acknowledgments

As always, thank you to my dear husband, Jim George, M.Div., Th.M., for your able assistance, guidance, suggestions, and loving encouragement on this project.

BECOMING A WOMAN OF BEAUTY & STRENGTH

Copyright © 2001 by Elizabeth George
Published by Harvest House Publishers
Eugene, Oregon 97402

ISBN-13: 978-0-7369-0489-6
ISBN-10: 0-7369-0489-1

Printed in the United States of America

08   09   10   11   12   13   / BP-CF /   18   17   16   15   14   13   12

Contents

Foreword

For some time I have been looking for Bible studies that I could use each day that would increase my knowledge of God's Word. In my search, I found myself struggling between two extremes: Bible studies that required little time but also had little substance, or studies that were in-depth and demanded more time than I could give. I discovered that I wasn't alone—there were many other women like me who were busy yet desired to spend quality time studying God's Word.

That's why I became excited when Elizabeth George shared her desire to create a series of women's Bible studies that offered in-depth lessons that could be completed in just 15-20 minutes per day. When she completed the first study—on Philippians—I was eager to try it out. I had already studied Philippians many times, but this was the first time I had come to understand exactly how the whole book fit together and how it can truly be lived out in my life. Each lesson was simple but insightful—and was written especially to apply to me as a woman!

In the Woman After God's Own Heart™ Bible study series, Elizabeth takes you step by step through the Scriptures, sharing wisdom she has gleaned from more than 20 years as a women's Bible teacher. The lessons are rich and meaningful because they're rooted in God's Word and have been lived out in Elizabeth's life. Her thoughtful and personable guidance make you feel as though you are studying right alongside her—as if she is personally mentoring you in the greatest aspiration you could ever pursue: to become a woman after God's own heart.

If you're looking for Bible studies that can help you grow stronger in your knowledge of God's Word even in the most demanding of schedules, I know you'll find this series to be a welcome companion in your daily walk with God.

—LaRae Weikert
Editorial Managing Director,
Harvest House Publishers

Before You Begin

In my book *A Woman After God's Own Heart™*, I describe such a woman as one who ensures that God is first in her heart and the Ultimate Priority of her life. Then I share that one crucial way this desire can become reality is by nurturing a heart that abides in God's Word. To do so means that you and I must develop a root system anchored deep in God's Word.

Before you launch into this Bible study, take a moment to think about these aspects of a root system produced by the regular, faithful study of God's Word:

- *Roots are unseen*—You'll want to set aside time in solitude—"underground" if you will—to immerse yourself in God's Word and grow in Him.

- *Roots are for taking in*—Alone and with your Bible in hand, you'll want to take in and feed upon the truths of the Word of God and ensure your spiritual growth.

- *Roots are for storage*—As you form the habit of looking into God's Word, you'll find a vast, deep reservoir of divine hope and strength forming for the rough times.

- *Roots are for support*—Do you want to stand strong in the Lord? To stand firm against the pressures of life? The routine care of your roots through exposure to God's Word will cultivate you into a remarkable woman of endurance.[1]

I'm glad you've chosen this study out of my A Woman After God's Own Heart™ Bible study series. My prayer for you is that the truths you find in God's Word through this study will further transform your life into the image of His dear Son and empower you to be the woman you seek to be: a woman after God's own heart.

In His love,

Elizabeth George

Setting the Scene

Esther 1:1-9

*E*sther! The name and story surrounding this famous and revered Old Testament queen evoke countless thoughts of character and courage. Even the Persian name, *Esther*, which means "star," creates anticipation of what's ahead of us. We'll be spending some exciting days together looking at the life of Esther, her beauty and strength, and her many "star qualities." But we don't actually meet Esther until our fourth lesson, so let's spend some time setting the scene for her entrance. Here are a few foundational facts to log before we step into the Bible's narrative recorded in the book of Esther:

Who wrote the book of Esther? The author is unknown. Some suspect Mordecai may have written it. Others suggest Ezra or Nehemiah. Whoever wrote Esther was most likely Jewish and quite familiar with King Ahasuerus and the events of his reign. (Also, just for your information, Esther is one of the two books of the Bible named after women, Ruth being the other.)

When was the book of Esther written? Estimates place the date between 464 and 424 B.C., but definitely following 465 B.C. when King Ahasuerus died. (And just a note—the events recorded in Esther fall between chapters 6 and 7 of the book of Ezra and close out the historical section of the Old Testament in your Bible.)

What is the theme of the book of Esther? Although the name of God is never mentioned, the book of Esther clearly shows us God's providential care and unfailing love for His people. As one has remarked, "If the name of God is not here, His finger is. He is in the shadows keeping watch over His own."

Where does the book of Esther take place? The story is set in the Persian Empire, and mostly takes place in Shushan (or Susa), the winter capital of the Persian court.

What are some of the problems encountered in studying the book of Esther? Some scholars critically point out that God is not mentioned (nor is prayer, worship, or God's law), and that Esther and her cousin Mordecai were not necessarily godly Jews (their ancestors had failed to return to Jerusalem when permitted, they agreed to keep Esther's Jewish identity secret, Esther probably ate foods that were unlawful for Jews, and Esther became a member of the king's harem). Nevertheless, most concede that both Mordecai and Esther demonstrated great courage and nobility and elements of high moral character.

Now let's see how Esther's story begins and launch our study of her many wonderful qualities.

Esther 1:1-9

[1] Now it came to pass in the days of Ahasuerus (this was the Ahasuerus who reigned over one hundred and twenty-seven provinces, from India to Ethiopia),

[2] in those days when King Ahasuerus sat on the throne of his kingdom, which was in Shushan the citadel,

[3] that in the third year of his reign he made a feast for all his officials and servants—the powers of Persia and Media, the nobles, and the princes of the provinces being before him—

[4] when he showed the riches of his glorious kingdom and the splendor of his excellent majesty for many days, one hundred and eighty days in all.

[5] And when these days were completed, the king made a feast lasting seven days for all the people who were present in Shushan the citadel, from great to small, in the court of the garden of the king's palace....

[9] Queen Vashti also made a feast for the women in the royal palace which belonged to King Ahasuerus.

From the Heart of God's Word...

1. List those who attended the 180-day banquet held by King Ahasuerus (verse 3). officals + servants, powers of Persia + Media, Nobles, + Princes

2. What is one thing King Ahasuerus did during these 180 days of feasting (verse 4)?
   Showed off... Everything showing his Money.

3. What people were invited to a second seven-day banquet (verse 5)? *All the People of shushan*

4. What was Queen Vashti doing during this time (verse 9)? *A feast for the women*

From Your Heart...

- Now that you've met King Ahasuerus, what are your first impressions of him?

- Like most kings, Ahasuerus had great wealth. But what does the Bible teach us about riches?

  Proverbs 30:7-9—

  Proverbs 31:20—

  Philippians 4:11-13—

  Which "school" of resources are you enrolled in today? Do you abound, or are you abased? Do you enjoy abundance, or are you doing without? Are you in plenty or in poverty? How do these scriptures encourage you?

- Consider this insightful statement...and then answer its penetrating question:

> *P*eople tend to admire four qualities in others: human wisdom, power (strength), kindness, and riches.... But God puts a higher priority on knowing him personally and living a life that reflects his justice and righteousness. What do you want people to admire most about you?[2]

Cultivating a Heart of Beauty & Strength

The scene is set. We've met several people—King Ahasuerus and his queen, Vashti. We've seen the scope of the king's empire—127 provinces stretching from India to Ethiopia. We've toured the palace and admired its furnishings. We've observed an extravagant feast (or two...or three!).

A little research reveals a few behind-the-scenes facts about this setting: King Ahasuerus was laying plans for an invasion of Greece. The six-month-long banquet afforded him a time to strategize with his princes and nobles as well as demonstrate the fact that he possessed the resources and wealth to wage a war. Furthermore, "for the majority of people in western Asia, then as now, life was hard and food none too plentiful. While laborers received barely enough to live on....life at court was extravagant beyond imagining."[3]

We'll see throughout the book of Esther that, although King Ahasuerus was used greatly by God, he was not a man of great character. And here in these few verses we see what someone has well observed—that "nothing hides a blemish so completely as cloth of gold."[4]

Dear one, we are not to be fooled by fortune and affluence. Neither are we to covet a life of wealth. We are called instead to be women after God's own heart, women who develop character. Therefore, *if you have plenty*, give liberally. Give generously and bountifully...and cheerfully (see 2 Corinthians 9:6-7). Seek to use God's blessings to bless others and to spend them for His eternal purposes. And, *if you have little*, seek contentment. Both situations provide opportunities for you and me to build godly character.

Losing a Beautiful Queen

Esther 1:10-22

*E*nglish poet John Keats penned that "a thing of beauty is a joy forever." Well, my friend, after finishing the lesson before us, you and I may well wonder, "...or is it?"

As we left off our last lesson on "Becoming a Woman of Beauty & Strength," we had just met Vashti, queen to King Ahasuerus. It will become quite obvious as we read on that Vashti was beautiful. Indeed her name meant "beautiful woman." And, in her own right, this queen possessed both strength and beauty. As the extended 180-day feast in the palace of the king progressed, displaying splendor beyond our imagination, it ultimately dissolved into drunken excess...with a disastrous outcome. Please be sure to read the passage in full in your own Bible. Then consider these few chosen verses, which adequately tell the tale.

Esther 1:10-22

¹⁰ On the seventh day, when the heart of the king was merry with wine, he commanded Mehuman, Biztha, Harbona, Bigtha, Abagtha, Zethar, and Carcas, seven eunuchs who served in the presence of King Ahasuerus,

¹¹ to bring Queen Vashti before the king, wearing her royal crown, in order to show her beauty to the people and the officials, for she was beautiful to behold.

¹² But Queen Vashti refused to come at the king's command brought by his eunuchs; therefore the king was furious, and his anger burned within him....

¹⁶ And Memucan answered before the king and the princes: "Queen Vashti has not only wronged the king, but also all the princes, and all the people who are in all the provinces of King Ahasuerus....

¹⁹ "If it pleases the king, let a royal decree go out from him, and let it be recorded in the laws of the Persians and the Medes, so that it will not be altered, that Vashti shall come no more before King Ahasuerus; and let the king give her royal position to another who is better than she.

²⁰ "When the king's decree which he will make is proclaimed throughout all his empire (for it is great), all wives will honor their husbands, both great and small."

From the Heart of God's Word...

1. *Request*—What was the condition of the king as he spoke to the eunuchs in charge of his royal harem on the final day of the additional week-long drinking feast (verse 10)?

And what was his request?

And what was his purpose?

2. *Response*—The next verses are filled with responses! What was that of Queen Vashti (verse 12)?

And of the king (verse 12)?

And of the spokesman for the king's wise men (verse 16)?

Repercussions—What personal consequences did Vashti suffer for her decision (verse 19)?

(As one has conjectured, perhaps the reasoning of the wise men went something like this—"If she will not come when summoned, let her not come ever again."[5])

And what reason was given for such a decree (verse 20)?

From Your Heart...

Before we make personal applications from this passage of Scripture and from the scene described, it will be helpful to know that "the laws of the Persians and the Medes" (verse 19) were irrevocable and could never be altered. That meant that once a law was written stating Vashti could no longer come before the king and that her royal position was to be given to another, it could never be changed or reversed.

• We've met King Ahasuerus. Now, what words would you use to describe him and his character?

• We've also met Queen Vashti. What words would you use to describe her?

- We've already learned that Queen Vashti was "beautiful to behold" (verse 11). So beautiful, in fact, that her husband wanted to show her (and her crown jewels) off. Many have guessed at why this beautiful queen chose not to honor her husband's request: Perhaps…

    …the men were drunk.
    …she was asked to appear in immodest clothing.
    …she was pregnant.

Whatever the reason, God has chosen not to let us in on it. And, as one writer comments on the omission of a reason, "Did the writer have some sympathy for Vashti and expect to evoke pity in his readers? He seems to have succeeded in doing so."[6]

What does Proverbs 22:1 say is more valuable than riches?

And Proverbs 11:16?

And Proverbs 31:25?

As you consider these truths about "beauty" and strength, what conclusions can you draw for your own values and conduct?

Cultivating a Heart of Beauty & Strength

Not knowing exactly why Vashti did not agree to her husband's request bothers a lot of people. Arguments rage on from the "For Vashti" side commending her refusal to degrade herself…to the "Against Vashti" side denouncing her conduct in refusing to submit to her husband.

But, dear reader, none of this debate matters. What matters is that God is at work here in the opening chapter of the book of Esther. We've already discussed the fact that God's name is never mentioned in this Old Testament book, yet His providential care and sovereign work are obvious as He's steadily at work in the shadows.

What's written in Proverbs 21:1—"The king's heart is in the hand of the Lord, like the rivers of water; He turns it wherever He wishes"—is true of the great, wealthy King Ahasuerus. Through a drunken mind, a refusal from a queen, the quick advice of a threatened man, and the agreement of a handful of counselors, God turned a king's heart...and a beautiful queen was removed. That's that—whether it was right or wrong. As Dr. Charles Swindoll writes,

> This is the wonder of God's sovereignty. Working behind the scenes, He is moving and pushing and rearranging events and changing minds until He brings out of even the most carnal and secular of settings a decision that will set His perfect plan in place.[7]

Now that God has opened up a vacancy at the top, let's see what happens next....

esson 3

Looking for a Queen

I'm sure you've done—or said—(or probably both!) some things that you later deeply regretted. As the classic saying goes, "to err is human." Each of us has, on occasion, made a hasty decision, spoken a speedy word, or succumbed to the crowd's influence.

Well, my friend, King Ahasuerus did all of the above. He made a hasty decision to dismiss his beautiful queen, Vashti. He spoke quickly an irrevocable edict to dethrone her. And he succumbed to the advice of others without pausing to think about potential results.

As we'll see in this lesson, it appears that King Ahasuerus came to regret his haste. Read along…and let's discover what happens next in the book of Esther.

Esther 2:1-4

¹ After these things, when the wrath of King Ahasuerus subsided, he remembered Vashti, what
she had done, and what had been decreed
against her.

² Then the king's servants who attended him said:
"Let beautiful young virgins be sought for the
king;

³ and let the king appoint officers in all the
provinces of his kingdom, that they may gather
all the beautiful young virgins to Shushan the
citadel, into the women's quarters, under the
custody of Hegai the king's eunuch, custodian
of the women. And let beauty preparations be
given them.

⁴ "Then let the young woman who pleases the
king be queen instead of Vashti." This thing
pleased the king, and he did so.

From the Heart of God's Word...

1. Record the first three words of Esther 2:1 here.

(It's significant to note that a lot of "things" happened
between the end of Chapter 1 and the first three words of
Chapter 2. About four years passed during that chapter
break, and some of the "things" the writer of Esther is
referring to include King Ahasuerus, also known as
Xerxes, going out to conquer Greece, and returning
home...badly defeated.)

As you read verse 1, what do you learn about the king's
moods? (Be sure to mentally add this information to what

you already know about the king's character and behavior.)

And what came to King Ahasuerus's mind as he thought affectionately upon Vashti?

2. Perhaps sensing the king's loneliness and discouragement...and regret, what suggestion did his counselors make (verses 2-4)?

(Just a note—Most scholars agree that the king's counselors were also acting in fear. They had contributed to the ousting of Vashti, and if she were restored as queen, she could punish them for their actions against her. Also it was possible that the king, too, might act against them if he continued to miss Vashti and began to blame his advisors for her removal.)

Describe the women to be sought (verses 2 and 3).

Describe the sweep of the search (verse 3).

What new person is introduced in verse 3, and what was his official function?

3. How did King Ahasuerus respond to this proposal and procedure (verse 4)?

From Your Heart...

• Can you think of a time when you were defeated in some major quest? When you were on top of the world...and then all seemed to topple? Perhaps reflecting on that time will help you relate to King Ahasuerus's situation.

- Everything to gain...and nothing to lose! That's King Aha-suerus! What would a kingdom-wide search for a queen cause the king to gain?

  (Just another note: A queen was usually selected from among political allies or from among the daughters of the counselors and advisors of the king. However, this queen would be selected for love and pleasure.)

- Our study is entitled *Becoming a Woman of Beauty & Strength*. We've already learned that Queen Vashti was "beautiful to behold" (Esther 1:11). Now we read that the king will choose a new queen from among the most beautiful women in his realm. Not only that, but the beauty of these women would be further enhanced by "beauty preparations" (verse 3). As we delve into an entire study about beauty, let's look right now at a few things God has to say about beauty. Take note...not only on paper here, but in your heart!

  1 Samuel 16:7—

  Proverbs 11:22—

  Proverbs 31:30—

Write out in a few sentences what it means to be beautiful in *God's* eyes. Also add one thing you can definitely do today to enhance God's brand of beauty in your life. And don't forget to spend time in prayer with Him about this most serious matter of beauty in *your* life!

Cultivating a Heart of Beauty & Strength

Four verses. That's all we've considered in this portion of our study…and yet many lessons are evident as we consider the political goings-on inside a king's castle. As we leave this quartet of scriptures, let's take these lessons with us:

Lesson One—God. It will be repeated over and over again throughout this study that whatever is happening in the book of Esther is a result of God at work in the shadows on behalf of His people. We can be sure that God planted the idea in the minds of the king's counselors to look for a queen that was outside the normal procedures and protocol. Thus a plan was hatched that threw the doors to the kingdom wide open for a "nobody" like Esther to walk through! (But…that's another lesson we must wait on!)

Lesson Two—Beauty. It's refreshing to be reminded of God's standards for true beauty. Faith and character—not external appearances—are what's important to God. He cares about your heart—not your hair, or your facial features, or your figure. Is yours a heart that finds favor with Him?

Lesson Three—Regret. We began our lesson with King Ahasuerus's regret over a hasty decision and action. I hope you find these words of advice helpful when it comes to your own decisions and actions!

Seven Things You'll Never Regret

Feeling reverence for your Maker.

Showing kindness to an aged person.

Destroying a letter written in anger.

Offering the apology that saves a friendship.

Stopping a scandal that could wreck a reputation.

Taking time to show loved ones consideration.

Accepting the judgment of God on any question.[8]

Lesson 4

Discovering "Diamonds in the Dust"

Esther 2:5-7

When my parents sold their almost-life-long home, they distributed their most treasured possessions among my three brothers and me. One of the cherished items I received was a pen-and-ink drawing of our family tree filled in with lovely hand-scripted calligraphy. I can look at this framed work at any time and visually chart my lineage. It's filled with who married whom, complete with wedding dates. Sons and daughters are noted, along with their wedding dates...and their sons and daughters....On and on my heritage stretches.

Well, dear one, today we get to observe the family tree of a very special family whom God had brought to a very special place for a very special time in history. It will be slightly

25

technical (as is any family tree), but I'll make it as simple as possible. First read how God reports the genealogy of two of His people.

Esther 2:5-7

⁵ Now in Shushan the citadel there was a certain Jew whose name was Mordecai the son of Jair, the son of Shimei, the son of Kish, a Benjamite.

⁶ Kish had been carried away from Jerusalem with the captives who had been captured with Jeconiah king of Judah, whom Nebuchadnezzar the king of Babylon had carried away.

⁷ And Mordecai had brought up Hadassah, that is, Esther, his uncle's daughter, for she had neither father nor mother. The young woman was lovely and beautiful. When her father and mother died, Mordecai took her as his own daughter.

From the Heart of God's Word...

1. First a few details from verse 5. Who is the man named?

And where did he live?

What specific details does God give about this man and his "family tree"?

(For your information, the Benjamites were the descendants of the patriarch Benjamin, the youngest son of Jacob and the grandson of Abraham—see Genesis 35:18, 22b-26. The Benjamites were one of the 12 tribes of Israel.)

2. As you read verse 6, what do you learn about Kish, the great-grandfather of Mordecai?

For a closer look at this tragic event, look at 2 Kings 24:13-16 and 2 Chronicles 36:9-10. Obviously, Mordecai (and his cousin Esther) was a direct descendant of one of the ten thousand leading citizens of Jerusalem who were taken as captives to Babylon.

Look also at 2 Chronicles 36:22-23. Mordecai's ancestors had not returned to Jerusalem after the fall of Babylon to Persia. Thus Mordecai came to be in Persia.

3. What do you learn about Mordecai in verse 7?

Referring to your answer, why?

How is Esther described physically?

What had happened to her parents?

(Just a note: *Hadassah* was Esther's Hebrew name, meaning "myrtle," and *Esther* was her Persian name, meaning "a star.")

From Your Heart...

• Take a look at your own family tree, dear friend. Have things gone in a perfect way for you and your ancestors? They hadn't for Mordecai, nor had they for Esther. Exiles and an orphan—these descriptions point to tragedy and heartbreak in their lives. How have you or your family or ancestors suffered?

- Words of comfort come streaming to us from God's Word to encourage us in our suffering. What strength do you find in these very few promises?

  Psalm 9:9—

  Psalm 18:2—

  Psalm 23:4—

  Psalm 46:1—

- We noted earlier that the name *Esther* means "star." And here, like the first twinkle of the evening star, we find the first ray of light in a pagan, godless land. The Bible's text to this point has been filled with scenes of wealth, pride, drunkenness and gluttony, betrayal, rage, and conniving politicians. Then suddenly...we meet the cousins Esther and Mordecai. They're Jews. They're God's chosen people. In this Jewish twosome, we see a glimmer of hope, a crack in the door to let a little light in on the darkness of the Persian world.

  This is an Old Testament story, but let's jump to the New Testament to see how we're to shine and influence this world of ours. What do you learn about the "light" you bring to those around you as a Christian?

  Matthew 5:16—

  Philippians 2:15—

  Ephesians 5:8—

- God is very careful throughout the Bible to preserve and to report the genealogy of His people, and that's what this passage of Scripture expounds—the genealogy of

Mordecai and Esther. A close look reveals that both Mordecai and Esther lacked family in their lives: Mordecai appears to have had no wife or children, and Esther had lost her parents...yet they had each other. They came to be where they were—in Persia—through the tragedy of captivity...yet they came to be in God's appointed place at just the right time to bring a beam of His light into a dark world.

God's sovereignty and providence is a watermark on every page of the book of Esther. And what is providence?

Providence...designates the continual care which God exercises over the universe which he has created.[9]

Do you, dear one, acknowledge God's power in *your* every circumstance, His plan for you *in* your every circumstance, and His divine purpose *for* your every circumstance? This would be a good time to spend time in prayer thanking your sovereign, all-powerful, loving God for the exercise of His continual care in each and every detail of your life.

Cultivating a Heart of Beauty & Strength

Just today a letter and a packet of note cards came in the mail from Joni Eareckson Tada. You're probably somewhat familiar with "Joni's Story." At age 17, Joni dove into a pond, hit an underwater object, and broke her neck. Paralyzed from the neck down, she has spent the last 25 years in a wheelchair. And yet, each note card displayed a lovely painting that this dear woman had drawn by holding pastel pencils clenched between her teeth!

What I especially loved about Joni's letter and cards—and what I kept thinking about during this lesson on the beauty and strength of Esther—was Joni's ability to find "diamonds in the dust" of her difficulties.[10] On the back of her leaflet she wrote these words:

> When I'm feeling inspired, there's nothing I enjoy more
> than wheeling up to my easel and working in pastels.
> It took years of practice, but I am thankful for good
> eyes and strong teeth so that I can praise the Lord
> through my artwork![11]

Can you, my friend, find even the smallest diamond—like a pair of good eyes or a set of strong teeth—in the dust of your difficulties? As someone has said, "Praising God for our blessings extends them. Praising God for our troubles ends them." Look your difficulties straight in the eye...and then lift loud, glorious, resounding praise to the throne of the Majesty on High!

Moving from the Mundane to the Mysterious

Esther 2:8-11

*I*n my book *Loving God with All Your Mind*, I wrote these words describing yet another woman of beauty and strength—Mary, the mother of our Lord Jesus Christ:

> The sun rose that morning just as it had risen every day of her life. As she ran through her list of chores, there was no hint that today her life would be transformed from the mundane to the mysterious. But something happened that day which changed everything—forever.[12]

As we consider what is about to happen to Esther, there are many similarities to this description of the day that changed Mary's life forever. First of all, Esther, too, was a young virgin. Second, Esther, no doubt, was living in obscurity, doing what she did every day of her life...when suddenly something happened that transformed her life and moved it from the mundane to the mysterious. Read on and step with the beautiful Esther into the king's palace.

Esther 2:8-11

⁸ So it was, when the king's command and decree were heard, and when many young women were gathered at Shushan the citadel, under the custody of Hegai, that Esther also was taken to the king's palace, into the care of Hegai the custodian of the women.

⁹ Now the young woman pleased him, and she obtained his favor; so he readily gave beauty preparations to her, besides her allowance. Then seven choice maidservants were provided for her from the king's palace, and he moved her and her maidservants to the best place in the house of the women.

¹⁰ Esther had not revealed her people or kindred, for Mordecai had charged her not to reveal it.

¹¹ And every day Mordecai paced in front of the court of the women's quarters, to learn of Esther's welfare and what was happening to her.

From the Heart of God's Word...

1. What startling event took place in Esther's life on one of her ordinary days (verse 8)?

   And under whose care was she placed (verse 8)?

2. Describe Esther's relationship with Hegai (verse 9).

Because of this relationship, what preferential favors did Esther receive (verse 9)? List them here.

3. As you read on in verse 10, what additional information do you learn about Esther?

4. Describe the loving concern of Mordecai for his cousin Esther (verse 11).

From Your Heart...

• Theories abound as to how Esther came to be "taken" into King Ahasuerus's palace. For instance, some say Mordecai aggressively entered her into the beauty contest as soon as he heard about it. Others paint a picture of Esther being physically dragged against her will into the palace. The Bible simply reports that she was "taken" to the palace complex.

  Can you point to any pivotal days in your life, dear one? A day and a happening that changed everything for you...and a day after which nothing would ever be the same? Some of us are "taken" aback by a phone call, or a knock on the door, or a letter arriving in the mailbox, or an appointment with a doctor or lawyer...signaling what Corrie ten Boom calls "the turning point."[13] In her own life, the turning point was a knock on her door by German soldiers. Her life turned from normal to horrendous as she entered a Nazi concentration camp on that day that began in the ordinary way. Describe your day.

• In Esther's case, God began to work *in* her difficult circumstance. Being taken into the king's palace and into this search for a queen meant that Esther would most likely never again leave the palace. If she pleased the king, she would be made queen and live in the palace. If she didn't become queen, she would pass the rest of her days as a concubine in the king's large harem.

Have you ever faced an uncertain future? Was your first reaction fear, worry, or surrender to God? And what did you do?

Upon arriving at the king's palace in Shushan, the region's most beautiful women were placed under the custody of Hegai, the king's chamberlain, the keeper of the women. This man was the chief eunuch and was "usually a repulsive old man, on whom the court ladies are very dependent, and whose favor they are always desirous to secure."[14]

What are some of the character qualities—sources of true beauty that perhaps Esther exhibited—that the Bible says wins favor with others...and God? (I know some of these are repeated from previous lessons—and they'll probably be repeated again—but it's most important that you and I, as women who desire the marks of *God's* beauty and strength on our lives, understand their importance to *Him*. You may want to use a dictionary to define some of these beautiful qualities.)

Proverbs 11:16—

Proverbs 31:10—

Proverbs 31:26—

Proverbs 31:30—

- It's obvious in these verses that the hand of God has moved once again on behalf of His people, causing Esther to find favor with the chief attendant of the women. Note two other Jews who ended up as strangers in a strange land against their will. What do you find to be true of their situations?

Genesis 37:26-28; 39:1-4—

Daniel 1:1-9—

How does God's oversight and loving care of these three oppressed people encourage you? Are you presently in a situation where you need to remember God's constant involvement in your life?

- Just one more issue to cover: Mordecai asked Esther not to reveal the fact that she was a Jew. There's also much speculation as to why he made this request. Yet, again, the Bible doesn't say. As we'll see throughout the book of Esther, Mordecai was a very wise man. Perhaps he...and Esther...were applying these principles of wisdom. Note them for yourself.

Proverbs 13:1—

Proverbs 13:3—

Cultivating a Heart of Beauty & Strength

Beauty is certainly more than mere looks. What we are on the inside always shines brighter than what we look like on the outside! Hegai, the eunuch, was surrounded by the region's most beautiful women. (It's estimated that the king's dragnet brought in up to 400 gorgeous women!) And yet, something in our star, Esther, shone brilliantly and drew Hegai's attention. Certainly it could have been her strength and beauty—the true beauty of strong character qualities. But, dear reader, it was also most definitely God's divine favor and superintendence in every detail of her difficult circumstance.   As I found in my notes from some now-unknown source, Esther received preferential treatment, defined as "practical advantages provided by God through others." What a wonderful truth for you and me to hold on to! Please write that humbling definition in your Bible or your journal—at least in the end cover of this book.

As I've prayed about the providence of God and how He moves us from the mundane to the mysterious, my mind moves immediately to Psalm 139 and God's encompassing love for us, His people. I believe there's no better way to end this lesson than to have you read Psalm 139 in your Bible and then declare along with the Psalmist, "Such knowledge is too wonderful for me; it is high, I cannot attain it" (Psalm 139:6).

Lesson 6

Preparing for an
Audience with the King

*J*live in Southern California, and, believe me, we're going
through a "spa craze"! It's very chic to take a day...or a
week...off and check yourself into a private spa tucked
away on a remote mountain or opening onto the Pacific
coastline. Specials run regularly on TV, listing not only the
regional top ten spa resorts, but the top ten in the world!
These ads show men and women sipping fruit smoothies,
dining on healthy cuisine from a veranda with a sweeping
view, soaking in hot mineral baths, being slathered with
mud body wraps, and enjoying facials, manicures, and pedi-
cures. And for those who can't afford the time off or the
money for such an outing, a take-home, do-it-yourself spa
treatment can be purchased in a box for $35!

But, my friend, *nothing* in this world in the way of spas and spa treatments will ever compare to what went on in Esther's day! For the details just read on in our Bible text.

Esther 2:12-15

¹² Each young woman's turn came to go in to King Ahasuerus after she had completed twelve months' preparation, according to the regulations for the women, for thus were the days of their preparation apportioned: six months with oil of myrrh, and six months with perfumes and preparations for beautifying women.

¹³ Thus prepared, each young woman went to the king, and she was given whatever she desired to take with her from the women's quarters to the king's palace.

¹⁴ In the evening she went, and in the morning she returned to the second house of the women, to the custody of Shaashgaz, the king's eunuch who kept the concubines. She would not go in to the king again unless the king delighted in her and called for her by name.

¹⁵ Now when the turn came for Esther the daughter of Abihail the uncle of Mordecai, who had taken her as his daughter, to go in to the king, she requested nothing but what Hegai the king's eunuch, the custodian of the women, advised. And Esther obtained favor in the sight of all who saw her.

From the Heart of God's Word...

1. Describe the "spa treatment" the women who were taken into the king's palace underwent in preparation for an audience with the king (verse 12).

2. What additional items were available to the young women for their appointment with the king (verse 13)?

3. After spending time with King Ahasuerus, to where was each woman returned and what was her hope (verse 14)?

4. When Esther's turn to go in to the king arrived, what did she ask for to enhance her appearance (verse 15)?

And what was the impression she made on all who saw her (verse 15)?

From Your Heart...

- Twelve months! Can you imagine...a whole year of preparation? The beauty treatment for these women and Esther consisted of being lotioned and perfumed—for twelve months!—with costly spices and fragrant oils and cosmetics. The intention was to cleanse and pluck, to bleach and lighten the color of the skin, to soften and perfume, and to remove spots and blemishes.

  But God has a more powerful and effective "beauty treatment" in mind for His women. Look at 1 Timothy 2:9-10, fill out the chart below indicating what's important to God, and enjoy the challenging thoughts below.

  DO be concerned about...   DON'T be concerned about...

*W*hile there is nothing wrong with Christian women wanting to look nice, each woman must examine her own motives. Today's world places great emphasis on beauty—exceptionally perfect women stare at us from magazine covers. Christian women, while they can dress nicely and take care of their appearance, must at the same time not let their appearance become all-encompassing....

A carefully groomed and well-decorated exterior is artificial and cold without inner beauty. Scripture does not prohibit a woman from wanting to be attractive. Beauty, however, begins inside a person. A gentle, modest, loving character gives a light to the face that cannot be duplicated by the best cosmetics and jewelry in the world. Christian women are not to try to be unattractive; instead, Paul called them to reject the world's standard for attractiveness. A Christian's adornment comes not from what she puts on, but from what she does for others.[14]

As a woman after God's own heart, do you need to place less emphasis on your external appearance and more emphasis on what's going on inside your heart? Jot down some thoughts about *how* a woman can nurture her heart (and make sure they are a part of your life, too).

Would others characterize you as a woman who is beautiful in good works? Spend time thinking about your ministries to others. (And don't forget to begin your list with your good works toward those who live right under your own roof!)

- Beauty…and strength. We've already been told that Esther was beautiful (Esther 2:7). In fact she was doubly blessed with beauty: She was "lovely" (meaning fair of form or shapely) and "beautiful" (meaning beautiful in countenance and face). And now she's undergone a full year of enhancing that God-given beauty. And yet, when it was time for Esther to appear before King Ahasuerus and she was given the opportunity to wear whatever she chose, who did Esther ask for advice and what did she do with that advice (verse 15)?

Here is remarkable beauty and strength! Instead of asking for expensive ornaments and jewelry and clothing (which many scholars believe the women were allowed to keep after being with the king), Esther asked for wisdom and advice from the one man who would best know the king's tastes. Look up these scriptures about the beauty of seeking…and taking…counsel.

Proverbs 12:15—

Proverbs 13:10—

Proverbs 15:22—

Proverbs 20:18—

Do you have a "corps of counselors"? Name those from whom you regularly seek advice. Also note how likely you are to take their advice.

What does Proverbs 28:26 say about the woman who trusts in her own knowledge?

- And once again, what was the result of Esther's consent to the counsel she was given even before she appeared before King Ahasuerus (verse 15)?

Cultivating a Heart of Beauty & Strength

Does Esther's opportunity sound like a Cinderella story? Well, don't get too excited! As tempting as such pampering and the chance to help herself to expensive treasures may sound, Esther and the other young women were merely concubines, the special possessions of the king, existing only for his pleasure.

And afterwards? After all of the beauty preparations and an all-night audience with the king, these women who were taken into the palace lived the remainder of their lives in the harem of concubines, where each spent the rest of her life in luxurious but desolate seclusion. None could leave the harem nor marry nor return to her family.[15]

Surely you and I should thank God for who we are, where we are, and what we have, rather than desire what looks and sounds advantageous in someone else's life! And surely we're blessed by not having our future solely dependent upon a one-night stand with a ruler. And surely, too, we should pay as much attention to our inward beauty as these women did to their outward beauty! Let's pray along with Socrates, the great Greek philosopher of old—"Grant that I may become inwardly beautiful."[16]

Here are a few of the ingredients in God's recipe for becoming inwardly beautiful:

#1. Determine what true beauty is—read the Bible.

#2. Desire it and pray for it.

#3. Diligently pursue it.

#4. Decide to ask for advice along the way.

Becoming Queen

Esther 2:16-18

*H*ow does a woman become queen? Usually by birth, heritage, privilege, and wealth. History resonates with the stories of individual women who were crowned queen because she brought political or financial advantage to her husband's position.

But God, the ever-present, all-powerful, ever-working guardian of His people, had other plans for Esther. And who was Esther? If her credentials were laid beside those of most queens, you would be tempted to answer, "Esther was nobody." So far, we've learned that Esther's résumé looked something like this:

✓ Jew   ✓ orphan
✓ cousin of Mordecai   ✓ lovely and beautiful

No, this meager, unimpressive list certainly offers no reason for Esther to ever become queen of any empire! In fact, there's no reason given here that would explain why a man like King Ahasuerus would even *know* a woman like Esther! ...Except for God's plan and God's providence. Let's read on and see what happens next....

Esther 2:16-18

¹⁶ So Esther was taken to King Ahasuerus, into his royal palace, in the tenth month, which is the month of Tebeth, in the seventh year of his reign.

¹⁷ The king loved Esther more than all the other women, and she obtained grace and favor in his sight more than all the virgins; so he set the royal crown upon her head and made her queen instead of Vashti.

¹⁸ Then the king made a great feast, the Feast of Esther, for all his officials and servants; and he proclaimed a holiday in the provinces and gave gifts according to the generosity of a king.

From the Heart of God's Word...

1. As we've noted, God keeps exacting records. What facts do we learn in verse 16 about what is taking place?

2. So much for the *historical* details! Now, what do we learn about King Ahasuerus's *emotional* response to Esther when she went in to him (verse 17)?

   And how did he show his admiration of Esther (verse 17)?

3. In what further way did King Ahasuerus express his joy (verse 18)?

Who was in attendance (verse 18)?

And how did those in the other 126 provinces enter into the king's celebration (verse 18)?

From Your Heart…

- *Regarding time*—Time had passed. Our study of the book of Esther reveals that 3½ to 4 years passed between Queen Vashti's dethronement for refusing to come before King Ahasuerus and Esther's appearance before the king. And time never stands still! Why? Because God is always at work. In the passing of time, the king's advisors mapped out a unique plan for choosing a new queen, a war was waged…and lost, and Esther spent a year in the palace beautification program.

  Is there any current area in your life where time seems to be standing still? Are you still "waiting" on graduation? Waiting for a husband? For children or grandchildren? For your husband's promotion at work? For needed finances? For a missions assignment? For an answer to prayer? As you consider the providence of God and His steady working in your waiting, what changes can you make in your thinking and in your attitude while you wait? In your attitude toward each new day, even the ordinary days?

  And how can you use the fact of God's supervision of the seconds, minutes, days and weeks…and years!…of your life to encourage someone else who's waiting?

- *Regarding favor*—God's providence is evident in the grace and favor He granted Esther in the sight of others. Esther found favor with Hegai (Esther 2:9), with all those who looked upon her (verse 15), and with King Ahasuerus (verse 17). She won the hearts of others, and now she's won the heart of the king. How do you view the blessings that come your way—preferential treatment, opportunities to serve the Lord, promotions, etc.? Do you "see" the hand of God at work? And do you make it a point to acknowledge and thank Him for each and every "favor"?

Look at Psalm 75:6-7. How can you be more sensitive to God's oversight of your life (and others' lives)?

Now look at Psalm 103:2. What can you do to be more aware of the Lord's "benefits" or kindnesses? The Knox translation declares, "Bless the Lord, my soul, remembering all he has done for thee." What can you do to "remember" the kindnesses of the Lord and to bless Him?

- *Regarding festivity*—Oh, was King Ahasuerus pleased with Esther! How proud he was of his beautiful new queen. So proud, in fact, that he gave a feast in her honor and called it "the Feast of Esther." There was a holiday of celebration and gift-giving. In many ways the message sent throughout the king's realm was loud and clear—a new queen, Queen Esther, was crowned and King Ahasuerus was delighted!

Cultivating a Heart of Beauty & Strength

Do you ever wonder about God's providence? The fact that God is always directing all things toward His end? As my pastor, John MacArthur, puts it, "Providence means that the hand of God is in the glove of human events."

In these beginning chapters of the book of Esther, we've witnessed the efforts of humans to impress, to direct, to rule, and to control. And yet, in and through these incidents, God has been using people, events, and circumstances to bring about His perfect will. You see, King Ahasuerus was never in control of His kingdom. And his counselors never had an original, bright idea about how to find a queen to please the king. And King Ahasuerus never chose Esther to be queen. God was simply using these people to direct all things toward His end—to preserve, protect, and care for His people. *God* crowned Esther queen...so that she, a parent-less Jewish girl could move inside the palace, not based on bounty and birthrights, but based on her God-given beauty. Our lesson could well be entitled, "*God* Selects a Queen."

Dear woman of beauty, as you and I seek God's kind of beauty and strength, there's none greater than a deep, abiding trust in Him. We must never panic, never fear, never wonder, never doubt, and never question *if* God is in control or *what* God is doing. True beauty and strength believes in the complete oversight of God, even over the minutia of life. We find His beauty as we rest in His providence, and His strength as we count on His providence.

Lesson 8

Informing the King

God works in many ways—as we've been learning in each lesson so far on the book of Esther. We've watched Him work in a large, dramatic way as when Vashti was removed from her throne. And in this lesson, we see Him work in an ordinary daily occurrence as Mordecai merely overhears two people in conversation. As we'll read here, Mordecai, the faithful cousin of Queen Esther, was himself a man of wisdom and strength. We've already witnessed the wise counsel and the loving care he gave to Esther, raising her, instructing her, checking up on her, and guiding her.

Even though Esther was a permanent resident of the palace, Mordecai was never too far away. We've caught a glimpse of Mordecai pacing outside the court of the women (Esther 2:11) and today we see him sitting in the king's gate...and getting an earful of information that forced him to act in loyalty and focuses our attention once again upon his strength and character.

Let's see exactly what happened on one of Mordecai and Esther's "ordinary days."

Esther 2:19-23

¹⁹ When virgins were gathered together a second time, Mordecai sat within the king's gate.

²⁰ Now Esther had not yet revealed her kindred and her people, just as Mordecai had charged her, for Esther obeyed the command of Mordecai as when she was brought up by him.

²¹ In those days, while Mordecai sat within the king's gate, two of the king's eunuchs, Bigthan and Teresh, doorkeepers, became furious and sought to lay hands on King Ahasuerus.

²² So the matter became known to Mordecai, who told Queen Esther, and Esther informed the king in Mordecai's name.

²³ And when an inquiry was made into the matter, it was confirmed, and both were hanged on a gallows; and it was written in the book of the chronicles in the presence of the king.

From the Heart of God's Word...

1. First, a few preliminaries: What is happening in verse 19?

And where was Mordecai?

Look again at Esther 2:10 and now at verse 20. What information is repeated?

And what reason is again given (verse 20)?

And what was Esther's response to Mordecai's advice (verse 20)?

2. No explanation for the second gathering of virgins in verse 19 is given. What is important follows: Who were Bigthan and Teresh (verse 21)?

And what did they do (verse 21)?

How did Mordecai, who either overheard these two men or was informed of their plans, handle the information (verse 22)?

How did Esther get involved (verse 22)?

3. Make a list of the order of events in verse 23.

From Your Heart...

- Esther is now *Queen* Esther...and yet what do we find her doing in verse 20?

How does this speak of her character?

Why do you think Esther still relied on Mordecai for advice?

Jot down here what Proverbs 13:14 says about the teaching of the wise—

And also Proverbs 19:20—

Are you a woman who is marked by the beauty and strength of heeding the advice of faithful, wise counselors? What changes must you make to gain this invaluable beauty mark?

Who are the faithful, wise counselors you depend on and look to for advice?

• Whenever you and I hear any information, we're forced to process it. We have to decide how to handle it, how to deal with it. We need wisdom in knowing whether to drop it, to forget it...or to act on it. This is the dilemma Mordecai faced—to tell or not to tell. And yet, in this case, Mordecai understood the seriousness and intensity of what he heard...and he acted! Again, what did he do?

And what did Esther do?

As you think about the beauty and strength of character exhibited by both Mordecai and Esther in this matter, what qualities come to mind?

What could they have done instead? (Don't forget what kind of person King Ahasuerus was!)

• This Old Testament illustration of authority and submission reminds us of a few New Testament passages that guide us in the area of our behavior toward those in authority. Make a few notes regarding these Scriptures:

Romans 13:1,7—

1 Peter 2:13-14—

1 Peter 2:17-18—

For another example of a man who faithfully served and honored his king, read Daniel 4:28-33. What kind of man was King Nebuchadnezzar, the man Daniel constantly cared for?

Give some thought to those who are "over" you in authority. Esther had her husband, Ahasuerus, and her cousin, Mordecai. Mordecai, too, was a man under authority—he served the king, actually sitting in the king's gate as an official in a position of prominence. Who are the people you're to serve and to honor in all faithfulness?

And how deep is your loyalty to them? Do you need to make any changes of heart? If so, what changes?

What exception does Acts 4:19-20 give to our loyal submission?

And Acts 5:29?

Cultivating a Heart of Beauty & Strength

As we seek to become women after God's own heart, you and I certainly have before us two invaluable traits to emulate in Esther *and* in her cousin Mordecai.

#1. Wise counsel—To be wise, we must seek the company of wise people. I've already mentioned a "corps of counselors." Do you yet have such a team? If not, don't give up! Instead, keep looking.

And keep praying, too! They're there. They just may not stand out from the crowd because another mark of wisdom is quietness—"Wisdom *rests quietly* in the heart of him who has understanding" (Proverbs 14:33, emphasis added), while a fool is always speaking out. Wisdom lays at rest in the heart of the one who has it, and, as yet another proverb instructs, "Counsel in the heart of man is like deep water, but a man of understanding will draw it out" (Proverbs 20:5)!

And never neglect to read. Many wise Christians and counselors have put their wisdom in writing. There's an abundant supply of good books that come from the hearts and minds of a multitude of wise men and women.

#2. Loyal commitment—King Ahasuerus was a difficult man...but he was Esther's husband and Mordecai's sovereign. Therefore they were loyal to him. Rather than see the king's murder as their "way out" of their own difficult, unchosen situation, they acted to save his life. Even though Esther had been "taken" away from Mordecai and into the king's palace (Esther 2:8), both were faithful to the lawful government and to the sovereign to whom they were subject.

As you seek to cultivate character in your life, seek wise counsel and live out loyal commitments to those you serve, whether at home or at work. Then you will walk in the beauty and strength of a woman after God's own heart.

Chasing the "Little Foxes"

Esther 3:1-6

*S*olomon, reported to be the wisest man who ever lived, wrote of "the little foxes that spoil the vines" (Song of Solomon 2:15). This saying points to the many little problems that can ruin something of bigger value. And certainly, in this lesson from the book of Esther, we see a little thing begin to topple a big man. Step into the Scriptures and take a look at a big little man.

Esther 3:1-6

¹ After these things King Ahasuerus promoted
   Haman, the son of Hammedatha the Agagite,
   and advanced him and set his seat above all the
   princes who were with him.

² And all the king's servants who were within the king's gate bowed and paid homage to Haman, for so the king had commanded concerning him. But Mordecai would not bow or pay homage.

³ Then the king's servants who were within the king's gate said to Mordecai, "Why do you transgress the king's command?"

⁴ Now it happened, when they spoke to him daily and he would not listen to them, that they told it to Haman, to see whether Mordecai's words would stand; for Mordecai had told them that he was a Jew.

⁵ When Haman saw that Mordecai did not bow or pay him homage, Haman was filled with wrath.

⁶ But he disdained to lay hands on Mordecai alone, for they had told him of the people of Mordecai. Instead, Haman sought to destroy all the Jews who were throughout the whole kingdom of Ahasuerus—the people of Mordecai.

From the Heart of God's Word...

1. A new chapter...and a new person. Whom do we meet for the first time in verse 1?

   And how was he honored by the king (verse 1)?

2. However, in verse 2 a problem arises! What was the king's command?

   And what was the conflict?

3. As the king's servants questioned Mordecai, what information did he reveal to them (verse 4)?

And what was Haman's response (verse 5)?

Rather than take his wrath out on one man, what course of action did Haman choose instead (verse 6)?

From Your Heart...

- *Haman*—Meet the king's new favorite! What do you learn about Haman's character from this lesson?

  (And, as a point of information, the word "destroy" or "wipe out" in verse 6 is used 25 times in the book of Esther. We'll soon see how Haman's desire to "destroy all the Jews who were throughout the whole kingdom of Ahasuerus—the people of Mordecai" unfolds as we work our way through the remaining chapters!)

- *Mordecai*—What do you learn about Mordecai's character from this lesson?

  There are several thoughts presented by scholars regarding Mordecai's actions. One is that Jews bowed to their kings, but when Persians bowed to another, it was the same as paying homage to a divine being. To see one such incident, look at Daniel 3:4-5,12. What answer did Daniel and his friends give to King Nebuchadnezzar in Daniel 3:18? Another view is that the Jews had a history of not bowing to their captors when in exile.

- *Esther*—It's true that Esther isn't a key player in this passage. But the wheels for drama and disaster are beginning to turn here in these six verses, movement that will definitely affect not only Mordecai, but also Esther...and all the Jews in the Persian Empire.

Cultivating a Heart of Beauty & Strength

As we look at Haman, we can't help but be amazed at how a "big" person can be so "little." Haman held the most prestigious position in the kingdom—second in command to the king. And yet he was reduced to seething hatred by one person, Mordecai. Filled with fury because of *one* man who won't bow to him, Haman stooped to plotting the annihilation of *all* the people of Mordecai.

In Haman we witness multiple negative traits. Anger, wrath, disdain, and hatred begin the list. His behavior forces us to ask of ourselves, "Is there any one person in my life whose behavior gets to me?" As Christians we're to put away anger (Ephesians 4:31). We're to forsake anger because of its devastating results. Marriages break up...because of anger. Families feud for decades...because of anger. Friends go their separate ways...because of anger. Churches split... because of anger.

Yet another proverb, Proverbs 19:11, speaks to the wise handling of a snub: "The discretion of a man makes him slow to anger, and it is to his glory to overlook a transgression." One mark of a truly "big" person is the ability to let some "little" things go, to overlook an offense, rather than allow the "little foxes to spoil the vines." In the New Testament, Philippians 4:5 says it this way: "Let your gentleness be known to all men." We're to let our forbearance, our humility, our sweet reasonableness, our magnanimity be obvious to everyone. In other words, we're to let a few things go by. Our "big"-heartedness should be easily recognized by all.

How are *you* doing so far, dear woman after God's own heart?

Anger is bad enough, but hatred is even more destructive. Haman's wrath turned into pure evil as he began to plan the elimination of Mordecai and all his people, the Jews. Little did Haman realize that in turning upon God's people, the Jews, he was provoking the wrath of God, for as God had written to His scattered and exiled people, "he who touches you touches the apple of His eye" (Zechariah 2:8).

How can you and I be truly "big" about the many "little" hurts in life? Or, how can we stop chasing the "little foxes"? Try these few tips to gain beauty and strength.

#1 Cultivate graciousness—"A gracious woman attains honor" (Proverbs 11:16).

#2 Choose a kind response—and put away "all bitterness, wrath, anger, clamor, and evil speaking" (Ephesians 4:31-32).

#3 Cleanse yourself—of any "little" root of bitterness that might spring up, cause you trouble, and defile you (Hebrews 12:15).

#4 Clothe yourself with love—along with tender mercies, kindness, humbleness of mind, meekness, and longsuffering (Colossians 3:12-14).

Plotting a Pogrom

Esther 3:7-15

*H*ang on, my friend! What you're about to read is neither beautiful nor admirable! You won't believe your eyes as you pore over the Bible text that comes next. It's awful! Terrible! Unimaginable! And cold-blooded! It's about the plotting of a pogrom. Is *pogrom* a new word for you? (It was for me.) It means bloodbath, holocaust, and massacre. It indicates butchery, carnage, and killing. It signifies slaughter and bloodshed. Consider yourself warned, utter a prayer, and...read on.

Esther 3:7-15

⁷ In the first month, which is the month of Nisan, in the twelfth year of King Ahasuerus, they cast Pur (that is, the lot), before Haman to determine

the day and the month, until it fell on the twelfth month, which is the month of Adar.

[8] Then Haman said to King Ahasuerus, "There is a certain people scattered and dispersed among the people in all the provinces of your kingdom; their laws are different from all other people's, and they do not keep the king's laws. Therefore it is not fitting for the king to let them remain.

[9] If it pleases the king, let a decree be written that they be destroyed, and I will pay ten thousand talents of silver into the hands of those who do the work, to bring it into the king's treasuries."

[10] So the king took his signet ring from his hand and gave it to Haman, the son of Hammedatha the Agagite, the enemy of the Jews.

[11] And the king said to Haman, "The money and the people are given to you, to do with them as seems good to you."...

[13] And the letters were sent by couriers into all the king's provinces, to destroy, to kill, and to annihilate all the Jews, both young and old, little children and women, in one day, on the thirteenth day of the twelfth month, which is the month of Adar, and to plunder their possessions.

[14] A copy of the document was to be issued as law in every province, being published for all people, that they should be ready for that day.

[15] The couriers went out, hastened by the king's command; and the decree was proclaimed in Shushan the citadel. So the king and Haman sat down to drink, but the city of Shushan was perplexed.

From the Heart of God's Word...

1. *Roulette*—Any dictionary defines the word *roul[* gambling game in which a marble is spun ar[*

inside of a bowl until the ball finally comes to rest in a numbered compartment, deciding the results of the wagers. Well, what takes place in verse 7 is a form of roulette, only the game was played with "Pur" or with a "lot," and the stakes were high...and evil. Read again Esther 3:6. What was the purpose for casting the lot in verse 7?

Who presided over the activity?

And when did this despicable deed take place?

2. *Request*—How did Haman describe the "certain people" to King Ahasuerus (verses 8)?

And what was Haman's conclusion regarding these "people" (verse 8)?

Ever the smooth politician, what did Haman suggest as a solution, and what further enticement did he include to sweeten the deal (verse 9)?

ponse—How did King Ahasuerus respond to Haman's osal (verse 10)?

erse 11?

niss it—How is Haman described in verse 10?

d, sealed, and delivered. These words 2-14. The decree for the massacre of the in all the languages of the people 's 127 provinces and then sealed with making it irreversible (see Esther ere sent out to carry the decree the kingdom. It's important for the decree's utter vileness, so write out what verse 13 says the people of the land were to do to the Jews.

5. *Repast*—With the deed done, what did King Ahasuerus and Haman do next (verse 15)?

And, in contrast, how did those in the city (Jews and non-Jews alike) handle the news?

(A point of information: The date for the Jewish blood-bath, which was determined by casting the lot, was set for 11 months later.)

From Your Heart...

- *Roulette*—Who do *you* think controls all things, including a date determined by the casting of the lot or rolling of dice? (For the correct answer, see Proverbs 16:33.)

- *Request*—Are *you* aware of how you can misrepresent the truth by using vagary, general terms, lies, and exaggeration? For a similar scenario, see Genesis 29:7-18.

- *Response*—King Ahasuerus's response to Haman's request was inept and exhibited incompetence, lack of interest, and unwillingness to determine the truth of the accusations. How do *you* usually respond to accusations against others? Do you check them out?

For an insight into the proper handling of such situations, see Proverbs 25:2.

- *Results*—The results of an evil heart that falsely accused innocent people and the lack of character in a leader literally sent shock waves throughout a vast empire. A pogrom was in progress! Read Proverbs 6:17-19 and list the six (no, make it seven) things God hates.

1.	5.
2.	6.
3.	7.
4.	

* *Repast*—How could these two men oh-so-casually sit down to drink after signing a death warrant for an entire race?! A better question is, how do *you* handle news of catastrophe befalling people?

For a few of God's instructions, see...

Proverbs 24:17—

Matthew 9:36—

Matthew 14:14—

Romans 12:15—

1 Corinthians 12:16—

Cultivating a Heart of Beauty & Strength

I know this was an involved passage, and a distressing one! But please read these wonderful words that point us to the more positive issue of God's providential care for His people.

The king and Haman sat down to drink. And so far as Haman was concerned, he did so with complete satisfaction, because he had now perfected his arrangements for the [elimination] of the Jews. There was, however, a quantity with which he had not reckoned, and that was that these people were the people of God. It is questionable whether he had any idea of such a fact; or, if he knew that these people claimed some special relationship with a God, he knew nothing of that God; nor thought it worthwhile to take such a matter into consideration. And thus he omitted the only factor of real importance....Therefore he sat down to drink with the king. And all the while Mordecai, the Jews, and Haman, were in the hands of God....[17]

Now, as a woman after God's own heart, take these lessons to heart for further developing a heart of beauty and strength:

1. Don't listen to gossip or slanderous statements.

2. If you happen to hear of some unusual behavior of someone you know, don't be too eager to believe it.

3. Be more compassionate and sensitive to the misfortunes of others.

esson 11

Weeping and
Wailing…and Warfare!

Esther 4:1-8

The wisdom book of Ecclesiastes declares, "There is a time to weep, and…a time to mourn" (Ecclesiastes 3:4). Well, dear reader, that "time" certainly arrived in the city of Shushan where Esther and Mordecai lived, as well as throughout the many provinces ruled by King Ahasuerus. But it appears that Mordecai was a man of action who went to battle against evil, even *as* he wept and mourned. Let's see what happened….

Esther 4:1-8

[1] When Mordecai learned all that had happened, he tore his clothes and put on sackcloth and

ashes, and went out into the midst of the city. He cried out with a loud and bitter cry.

² He went as far as the square in front of the king's gate, for no one might enter the king's gate clothed with sackcloth.

³ And in every province where the king's command and decree arrived, there was great mourning among the Jews, with fasting, weeping, and wailing; and many lay in sackcloth and ashes.

⁴ So Esther's maids and eunuchs came and told her, and the queen was deeply distressed. Then she sent garments to clothe Mordecai and take his sackcloth away from him, but he would not accept them.

⁵ Then Esther called Hathach, one of the king's eunuchs whom he had appointed to attend her, and she gave him a command concerning Mordecai, to learn what and why this was.

⁶ So Hathach went out to Mordecai in the city square that was in front of the king's gate.

⁷ And Mordecai told him all that had happened to him, and the sum of money that Haman had promised to pay into the king's treasuries to destroy the Jews.

⁸ He also gave him a copy of the written decree for their destruction, which was given at Shushan, that he might show it to Esther and explain it to her, and that he might command her to go in to the king to make supplication to him and plead before him for her people.

From the Heart of God's Word...

1. In our previous lesson, we looked at how Haman and King Ahasuerus responded to the decree calling for the

death of all Jews in the land: After it was sent out, they sat down to drink (Esther 3:15). We also noted the general response of the people in the city of Shushan where the announcement was made first—they were perplexed. From Esther 4:1 and 2, describe Mordecai's response.

And how did the Jews throughout the provinces respond (verse 3)?

2. And what did Esther's maids and eunuchs do when they learned of Mordecai's mourning (verse 4)?

What action did Esther take (verse 4)?

And what did Mordecai do (verse 4)?

3. Because Esther and Mordecai couldn't speak directly to each other, one of the eunuchs, Hathach, became a message-bearer. What message(s) and instructions did Mordecai send to Esther through Hathach (verse 7)?

From Your Heart...

In these dismal scenes of alarm and mourning, we see a mass of people responding physically and emotionally with much weeping and wailing! However, someone had to take action. Even in the midst of weeping and wailing, *someone* had to go to war! *Someone* had to do *something*!

• What actions did Mordecai take?

• What actions did Esther take?

How do you think Esther exhibited strength and beauty of character as a woman?

- When life strikes a blow against you or your loved ones, are you prone to emotional responses only, or do you move into action? Do you tend to do nothing, or do you do something? Do you let things happen, or do you put on your battle gear, go to war, and try to make some difference? After you answer these questions, think about where you fit in the equation below.

> *P*eople can be divided into three groups: those who make things happen, those who watch things happen, and those who wonder what happened.[18]

Cultivating a Heart of Beauty & Strength

Our study, dear one, is all about character, about nurturing strong traits, about developing powerful inner qualities, qualities that qualify you to be known as a woman after God's own heart.

And yes, we need emotion, too. We've just witnessed two people who had no emotion—King Ahasuerus and Haman. A lack of emotion is a lack of heart, inhuman!

But you and I also need to take action when action is called for, not just watch and wonder at what's happening! Action is a mark of the "strength" we're learning about in our quest to become women of beauty and strength.

- Action signals the beautiful presence of courage, the ability to think...and act...under duress.

- Action also speaks of values. It means we value something enough to try rather than tire, to get up and go on rather than give up.

- Action also exhibits faith. Only a strong trust in God can enable us to go to war and fight for what's right.

Esther and her cousin Mordecai show us emotion—they wept and wailed. But they also show us action in that they refused to sit and mourn while this life-and-death situation unfolded. They rolled up their sleeves and went to war.

We'll see more about their joint "battle plan" in the next lesson, but as we wait to turn the page, consider the heartbreak of Nehemiah (cupbearer to King Ahasuerus's son several decades after the events of Esther) when he heard about enemy assaults against God's people in Jerusalem. You see, there were no walls around the city. And what was Nehemiah's response to the distressing news about his people? It was emotional! He writes,

So it was, when I heard these words, that I sat down and wept, and mourned for many days; I was fasting and praying before the God of heaven" (Nehemiah 1:4).

However, Nehemiah, although deeply grieved about the condition of Jerusalem, didn't just brood about it. After his initial grief, he prayed, pouring out his heart to God (Nehemiah 1:5-11), and he looked for ways to improve the situation. Nehemiah put all his knowledge, experience, and organizational skills into determining what should be done.

When tragic news comes to you, first pray. Then seek ways to move beyond grief to specific action that helps those who need it.[19]

Lesson 12

Choosing at the Crossroads

Esther 4:9-17

I love the title of a book written about Esther by Jeanette Lockerbie—*Esther, Queen at the Crossroads.*[20] A crossroad is the place where two or more roads intersect. And, as you well know, whenever we approach an intersection of roads, a choice must be made. Direction must be determined.

Esther 4:9-17

⁹ So Hathach returned and told Esther the words of Mordecai.

¹⁰ Then Esther spoke to Hathach, and gave him a command for Mordecai:

71

11 "All the king's servants and the people of the king's provinces know that any man or woman who goes into the inner court to the king, who has not been called, he has but one law: put all to death, except the one to whom the king holds out the golden scepter, that he may live. Yet I myself have not been called to go in to the king these thirty days."

12 So they told Mordecai Esther's words.

13 Then Mordecai told them to answer Esther: "Do not think in your heart that you will escape in the king's palace any more than all the other Jews.

14 "For if you remain completely silent at this time, relief and deliverance will arise for the Jews from another place, but you and your father's house will perish. Yet who knows whether you have come to the kingdom for such a time as this?"

15 Then Esther told them to reply to Mordecai:

16 "Go, gather all the Jews who are present in Shushan, and fast for me; neither eat nor drink for three days, night or day. My maids and I will fast likewise. And so I will go to the king, which is against the law; and if I perish, I perish!"

17 Then Mordecai went his way and did according to all that Esther commanded him.

From the Heart of God's Word...

1. Briefly relate the law regarding coming before the king and its exception (verse 11).

   How long had it been since Esther had seen King Ahasuerus (verse 11)?

What risk would Esther be taking to approach the king (verses 11 and 16)?

2. In verse 13, what reminder did Mordecai give Esther?

What were Mordecai's beliefs regarding the deliverance of the Jews (verse 14)?

And what was his final appeal to Esther (verse 14)?

3. As Esther agreed to Mordecai's advice, what did she ask of him (verse 16)?

Write out Esther's famous words of strength and courage that have lived down through the centuries (verse 16).

From Your Heart...

Esther: Queen at the Crossroads! Would she "remain completely silent at this time" (verse 14), or would she "go in to the king to make supplication to him and plead before him for her people" (verse 8)? Ever the woman of both beauty and strength, Esther chose the path of action.

• Esther responded to Mordecai's challenge that she was involved in an event that was larger than herself—the lives of her people, the Jews, were at stake! What are the events that are larger than yourself, who are the people involved, and what sacrifices are you making or are willing to make for their welfare?

• Esther made war with good advice. Once again, what does Proverbs 20:18 say?

How important do *you* think it is to act on the good advice given by others? And why?

- Is there any situation, belief, purpose, or person for which you, too, would utter, "If I perish, I perish!" as you move into battle? Explain your answer.

- We have witnessed all sorts of beauty preparations throughout the book of Esther. Esther herself had previously experienced an intensive physical beauty treatment. But now, as she prepares to take the risk of approaching her husband, the king, she undergoes a completely different kind of "beauty treatment"—an internal one. What were the elements of her preparation, and why do you think she included each?

  Also note Proverbs 15:28 with respect to preparation—

  (Just a note about prayer and fasting: While neither prayer nor God is ever mentioned in the book of Esther, most scholars believe that prayer to God is obviously implied in Esther's decision to fast, for fasting without prayer to God would have been useless.)

Cultivating a Heart of Beauty & Strength

Our Esther arrived at the crossroads. And because she chose the harder path of action, her beauty and strength shine all the brighter! What are some of the brilliant lessons her "crossroads" experience teaches us as women who seek the evidence of God's beauty and strength in our lives?

1. *Know the proper purpose...*what's important. The situation Esther faced was bigger than herself. And Esther hands down a lesson in beauty and strength to you and

me: Know what very few great issues are worth a war! Obviously we can't go to war over everything, nor should we. A woman of beauty and strength has the wisdom and discernment to know what's important and what's not, what's big and what's little, what has a grand purpose and what's minuscule. For the important, big, and grand purposes, she will risk all!

2. *Know the proper timing. Now* was the time for Esther to reveal to her husband, King Ahasuerus, that she was a Jew. Perhaps you've wondered why Esther's heritage was kept secret from the king. However, regardless of whether withholding that knowledge was right or wrong is no longer important. It is abundantly clear that *now* was the time to make it known. And, whether keeping that information to herself was right or wrong, we're going to see God mightily use the revelation of that fact in the days to follow.

3. *Know the proper preparations.* What's the old saying, "Fools rush in where angels fear to tread"? Our Esther certainly didn't rush in and hysterically throw herself before her difficult husband, the tyrannical King Ahasuerus! No! She waited and prayed and fasted. And she drew upon the support of others, too.

Whenever you stand at life's crossroads, remember your choices: Will you choose to be passive...or to act in passion? Will you choose what is easy...or what is hard? Will you choose the low road of selfishness...or the high road of beauty and strength? Your choices will determine your character!

*L*esson 13

Turning Point to Greatness

Esther 5:1-8

*A*s you'll soon see, there's been a turning point in the book of Esther. Although Esther is queen, her guardian and cousin, Mordecai, has been faithfully advising her from a distance. However, as we ended Chapter 4, Esther uttered her most famous words, "If I perish, I perish." And, after asking that the local Jews fast for three days on her behalf, she retreated to do the same.

And today, ah! Today, the noble Esther strides out of the shadows and onto the stage of greatness. No longer is Mordecai in charge of things, but our Esther boldly and beautifully steps up to the responsibility of speaking up on behalf of her people to her husband, the king. *Her* time to act has arrived. *She* is the one on the inside of the palace, the one in position "for such a time as this." It is her moment to be the "star" that her name indicates. The baton of command has been passed from Mordecai to Esther! And she courageously takes on the task and moves forward in full dignity.

Do you want to see what a strong and beautiful woman looks like? Well, dear one, take note! In Esther we witness a parade of virtues. This is her finest hour. Yes, she dons the royal robes as queen. But don't fail to notice the many radiant facets of her character.

Esther 5:1-8

¹ Now it happened on the third day that Esther put on her royal robes and stood in the inner court of the king's palace, across from the king's house, while the king sat on his royal throne in the royal house, facing the entrance of the house.

² So it was, when the king saw Queen Esther standing in the court, that she found favor in his sight, and the king held out to Esther the golden scepter that was in his hand. Then Esther went near and touched the top of the scepter.

³ And the king said to her, "What do you wish, Queen Esther? What is your request? It shall be given to you—up to half my kingdom!"

⁴ So Esther answered, "If it pleases the king, let the king and Haman come today to the banquet that I have prepared for him."

⁵ Then the king said, "Bring Haman quickly, that he may do as Esther has said." So the king and Haman went to the banquet that Esther had prepared.

⁶ At the banquet of wine the king said to Esther, "What is your petition? It shall be granted you. What is your request, up to half my kingdom? It shall be done!"

⁷ Then Esther answered and said, "My petition and request is this:

⁸ "If I have found favor in the sight of the king, and if it pleases the king to grant my petition and fulfill my request, then let the king and Haman come to the banquet which I will prepare for them, and tomorrow I will do as the king has said."

From the Heart of God's Word...

1. *Phase 1*—The time of preparations was over—it was "the third day." Almost 40 hours of praying and fasting were complete. And now it was time for Esther to move forward and act! Consider these words, and then we'll "move forward" ourselves.

> *G*od was in control, yet...Esther had to decide to act. We cannot understand how both can be true at the same time, and yet they are. Possibly it is because God chooses to work through those *willing* to act for him. We should pray as if all depended on God and act as if all depended on us. We should avoid two extremes: doing nothing and feeling that we must do it all.[21]

2. How did Esther care for her appearance (verse 1)?

What was her next course of action (verse 1)?

Imagine the drama, the tension, the risk of it all as we remember that Esther had not been called to come before the king for over a month, and that anyone who approached him uninvited died...unless the king extended his scepter to that person. As Josephus, the early Jewish historian, wrote of the Persian king, "Round his throne stood men with axes to punish any who approached the throne without being summoned."[22] It was a serious situation for Esther! Had she fallen into disfavor with the king? Had he written her off as a favorite? Was he enjoying the pleasure of another woman? Had he perhaps heard that she was Jewish? As you can see, there were many factors in the equation that would determine whether or not Esther would live or die!

Finally, after all of the preparations (don't forget to notice verse 4!) and prayer and fasting, Esther stood in the court. What was she wearing (verse 1)?

What reception did she receive from the king (verse 2)?

3. *Phase 2*—Knowing that Esther had risked her life to speak to him, what did the king immediately ask (verse 3)?

And what was Esther's request (verse 4)?

How did King Ahasuerus respond to her request (verse 5)?

4. *Phase 3*—At Esther's carefully prepared banquet of wine, what did her husband, the king, again ask (verse 6)?

And what was Esther's reply (verse 8)?

From Your Heart...

- *Phase 1*—After considering this passage and the events as they unfold, what difference do you think her choice of clothing might have made?

As a bit of well-known advice heralds, "You never get a second chance to make a good first impression!" Esther, our heroine of beauty and strength, paid close attention to her selection of clothing. How carefully do you plan and choose what you wear? Is this perhaps an area you need to pay more attention to?

- *Phase 2*—What do you learn from Esther's approach to her problem in these areas?

Her speech patterns toward her husband? Esther's words were appropriate for her day and for addressing royalty (a lesson in and of itself!). But what else can you learn?

Her preparations?

Her plan?

- *Phase 3*—What do you learn from Esther's further actions in these areas?

Her second plan?

Her choice to wait?

Her ability to wait?

Cultivating a Heart of Beauty & Strength

This is indeed a practical passage! Here God allows us to witness firsthand the fruits of many of the disciplines we seek to faithfully practice.

The fruits of prayer and fasting. Esther stepped up to her challenge with a clear head and a clear plan, and was clearly courageous. Time (indeed, three days of it) spent in prayer and fasting had given Esther practical solutions, emotional calmness, and a blazing faith.

The fruits of waiting. Our Esther didn't blurt out her request, but instead invited the king and his friend Haman to a drinking feast. Sensing that the timing for her request wasn't quite right, Esther wisely waited even longer. Also, the king had been drinking, and Esther prudently followed one of the cardinal rules of dealing with someone who's been drinking, and that is to wait until they're sober to talk about important matters. (For another example, see Abigail's situation in 1 Samuel 25, especially verses 36-37.)

The fruits of beauty and strength. Yes, Esther looked beautiful in her carefully selected clothing, but her beautiful virtues were on parade, too. My personal list of Esther's excellent qualities includes faith, determination, purpose, and resolve. Not only was she cool and calm, but she acted with wisdom and discernment, spoke with sweet speech and confidence, and carried out her plans with courage, assurance, and valor.

Now...what does your parade of virtues look like? And remember, as you practice these virtues in your life, you, too, will be ready for your turning points to greatness as a woman of beauty and strength.

Taking the High Road

*I*n Lesson 9 we considered "the little foxes that spoil the vines" (Song of Solomon 2:15). Well, today we meet "the fly in the ointment." As Solomon also wrote, "Dead flies putrefy the perfumer's ointment, and cause it to give off a foul odor" (Ecclesiastes 10:1).

Haman, the villain in God's account of the persecution of His people, had it made! He had been promoted to the highest position in the land (Esther 3:1). In fact, everyone in the king's gate was commanded to bow before Haman (Esther 3:2). However...there was one fly in the ointment of Haman's sweet success, one person who wouldn't bow down to him, one man who was ruining Haman's triumph. Take heed as you read on!

Esther 5:9-14

⁹ So Haman went out that day joyful and with a glad heart; but when Haman saw Mordecai in the king's gate, and that he did not stand or tremble before him, he was filled with indignation against Mordecai.

¹⁰ Nevertheless Haman restrained himself and went home, and he sent and called for his friends and his wife Zeresh.

¹¹ Then Haman told them of his great riches, the multitude of his children, all the ways in which the king had promoted him, and how he had advanced him above the officials and servants of the king.

¹² Moreover Haman said, "Besides, Queen Esther invited no one but me to come in with the king to the banquet that she prepared; and tomorrow I am again invited by her, along with the king.

¹³ Yet all this avails me nothing, so long as I see Mordecai the Jew sitting at the king's gate."

¹⁴ Then his wife Zeresh and all his friends said to him, "Let a gallows be made, fifty cubits high, and in the morning suggest to the king that Mordecai be hanged on it; then go merrily with the king to the banquet." And the thing pleased Haman; so he had the gallows made.

From the Heart of God's Word...

1. How did Haman feel after Esther's banquet (verse 9)?

And what happened to change his mood (verse 9)?

2. What was Haman's next act (verse 10)?

Jot down Haman's list of "bragging rights" (verses 11-12).

(Also jot down what Proverbs 12:23 says!)—

3. Yet, in Haman's own words, all of his blessings meant nothing! Why (verse 13)?

What did Haman's wife and friends propose (verse 14)?

And how did Haman respond to their advice (verse 14)?

And how quickly was the deed done (verse 14)?

(Just a note: Mordecai was scheduled to die in the pogrom anyway. It appears that Haman couldn't wait until the appointed date of the massacre!)

From Your Heart...

• *One person!* That's all it took to ruin Haman's day! Is there any one person that you allow to spoil the sweetness of your days, just as a single fly ruins the fragrance of perfume?

Have you allowed any destructive and sinful attitudes or actions toward this person to take root in your heart (see Hebrews 12:14-15)? If so, what words does Jesus have in Luke 6:27-28 for our godly response toward our "enemies"?

First, Jesus' general command is to...

Next, toward those who hate us, we are to...

And, toward those who curse us, we are to...

And, toward those who despitefully use us, we are to...

Be sure you spend time in prayer asking for God's help in living with such difficulties *His* way!

- *One group!* That's all it took to seal Haman's fate! Throughout our study, we've considered the value of a wise corps of counselors. Well, today we meet Haman's corps of counselors. Based on their advice, how would you characterize them?

- *One woman!* That's all it took to push Haman over the edge! We'll see the results of Haman's wife's advice soon, but today let's take a hard look at some other wives who influenced their husbands for the worse. Scan these scriptures and note the advice given and/or the action taken.

  Eve (Genesis 2:16-17; 3:6)—

  Jezebel (1 Kings 21:1-4,7,15)—

  Sapphira (Acts 5:1-2,9-10)—

  What do these proverbs have to say about wives?

  Proverbs 12:4—

  Proverbs 14:1—

  Proverbs 18:22—

  Proverbs 19:14—

  Proverbs 31:11-12—

  If you're a wife, do you find any areas for needed improvement in these verses?

- *One final exercise!* Contrast Esther's qualities and causes
  with those of Zeresh, Haman's wife.

Esther	Zeresh

Cultivating a Heart of Beauty & Strength

In art, it's the dark hues that cause the more brilliant ones to
stand out. Well, we certainly see that reality in the lesson
before us. For at least three full chapters, we've seen the
beauty and strength of not only Esther, but also of her rela-
tive Mordecai. My, how they shine in the dark days of the
book of Esther!

But today we can't help but notice the murky tones of
another family. Haman, his wife, and their gang of lowlifes
are certainly flies in the ointment! They're putrid and "stink"
(as The Living Bible says of dead flies) compared to the
sweet aroma surrounding Esther and Mordecai.

I've been mentally contrasting these two families....

—Mordecai was a faithful friend, guardian, and advisor as
he pushed Esther to do the right thing, regardless of the cost.
Proverbs 27:5 and 6 teach us that open rebuke and the
faithful wounds of a friend are better than false love.
Haman's gang, on the other hand, failed to bring out the
best in him.

—Esther and Mordecai were toiling at a great price to
save the lives of an entire people, while Haman and his
henchmen (led by his wife) were hatching plans not only to

murder all Jews, but now specifically (and dramatically—a gallows 50 cubits high measured 75 feet high, the equivalent of a eight-to-ten-story building!) to execute Mordecai.

—The virtues that make up the beauty and strength of Esther and Mordecai arch as a radiant rainbow through the skies of such dark times, while Haman and his crew sink lower and lower to traits of a shadier, more sinister nature.

We've noted before the importance of every choice we make, and in these two families we see the good, the bad... and the ugly(!)...lived out through decisions made. The words of this poem are all too true! Please, as a woman of beauty and strength, take the high road!

To every man there openeth
A Way, and Ways and a Way.
And the High Soul climbs the High Way
And the Low Soul climbs the Low,
And in between, on the misty flats,
The rest drift to and fro.
But to every man there openeth
A High Way and a Low;
And every man decideth
The Way his soul shall go.[23]

—John Oxenham

Spending a Sleepless Night

Esther 6:1-9

*H*ave you ever done a good deed...only to have it go unnoticed? Well, that's exactly what happened to Esther's cousin Mordecai. As you remember, Mordecai overheard a plot to kill the king and reported it. And sure enough, an investigation revealed that the plot was real, the two culprits were executed, and Mordecai's noble act "was written in the book of the chronicles in the presence of the king" (Esther 2:23)...and promptly forgotten.

Today we'll learn at least three life lessons: First, the beauty of being content when overlooked; second, the beauty of godly humility; and third, the beauty of God's providential oversight of His people and supervision of all things. So let's step into Chapter 6 of Esther and see what God has for us...and Mordecai...and Haman.

Esther 6:1-9

¹ That night the king could not sleep. So one was commanded to bring the book of the records of the chronicles; and they were read before the king.

² And it was found written that Mordecai had told of Bigthana and Teresh, two of the king's eunuchs, the doorkeepers who had sought to lay hands on King Ahasuerus.

³ Then the king said, "What honor or dignity has been bestowed on Mordecai for this?" And the king's servants who attended him said, "Nothing has been done for him."

⁴ So the king said, "Who is in the court?" Now Haman had just entered the outer court of the king's palace to suggest that the king hang Mordecai on the gallows that he had prepared for him.

⁵ The king's servants said to him, "Haman is there, standing in the court." And the king said, "Let him come in."

⁶ So Haman came in, and the king asked him, "What shall be done for the man whom the king delights to honor?" Now Haman thought in his heart, "Whom would the king delight to honor more than me?"

⁷ And Haman answered the king, "For the man whom the king delights to honor,

⁸ let a royal robe be brought which the king has worn, and a horse on which the king has ridden, which has a royal crest placed on its head.

⁹ Then let this robe and horse be delivered to the hand of one of the king's most noble princes,

that he may array the man whom the king delights to honor. Then parade him on horseback through the city square, and proclaim before him: 'Thus shall it be done to the man whom the king delights to honor!' "

From the Heart of God's Word...

1. How did King Ahasuerus spend the night after Esther's dinner (verse 1)?

   As the king listened to the records of the chronicles, what information caught his attention (verse 2)?

2. When the king asked, "What honor or dignity has been bestowed on Mordecai for this?" what was the answer (verse 3)?

3. What did the king ask of Haman when he arrived at the palace? (verse 6)?

   And what was his lengthy(!) answer (verses 7-9)? And why (verse 6)?

From Your Heart...

- *Prizes*—During the five years of failing to be rewarded with some kind of prize and praise, Mordecai continued to faithfully serve the king. (Every time we read that Mordecai "sat in the king's gate" [Esther 2:21; 3:2; 5:13], it means that he was probably an official who was dispensing his responsibilities, perhaps a magistrate or a judge.) Now think about yourself. Are you one who needs recognition and prizes for deeds done, or could you go unthanked for five years...or forever?

What truth about rewards and prizes does Jesus give us in Matthew 6:6?

A good question to ask yourself is, "Why do I do what I do?" And the answer...?

- *Pride*—Oh, is this glimpse into the heart of Haman awful! He, too, hadn't slept. But, instead of working on a plan for *honoring* a loyal subject who had been overlooked for his courage, Haman had been up all night working on his evil plan, feverishly supervising the construction of the outrageously high gallows meant for *hanging* Mordecai. When asked about how *he* would honor a faithful servant, Haman opened his mouth...and out spouted a stream of over-confidence and self-glorification and exaggerated exaltation. What do these verses teach us about the ugliness (and danger!) of pride and the beauty of humility?

    Proverbs 11:2—

    Proverbs 16:18—

    Proverbs 18:12—

  How can you put the truths—and promises!—of 1 Peter 5:5-6 to work in your service to others?

- *Providence*—We'll take a longer look at God's providence in our next lesson, but for now we must, along with most Old Testament scholars, attribute the fact that King Ahasuerus couldn't sleep to the fact that *God* prevented him from sleeping. How did another king spend a sleepless night in Daniel 6:16-23?

  How did Jacob spend his sleepless night in Genesis 32:24-32?

What seem like coincidences might actually be God-incidents. Next time you can't sleep, consider that God might be trying to get your attention. How could you respond to a God-ordained sleepless night?

Cultivating a Heart of Beauty & Strength

What an intriguing passage from the Bible! It's filled with awful people, awful acts, and yet contains so many beautiful lessons for you and me, dear reader, if we will just *remember...*

Prizes—When your good deeds are overlooked, *remember* that *God* knows all about it, and *He* will reward you richly in the days to come. As the New Testament exhorts, "let us not grow weary while doing good, for in due season we shall reap if we do not lose heart. Therefore, as we have opportunity, let us do good to all, especially to those who are of the household of faith" (Galatians 6:9-10).

Pride—At every opportunity, *remember* the beauty of a humble heart and how God treasures it. God's prophet Micah reminded the people of his day, "He has shown you, O man, what is good; and what does the Lord require of you but to do justly, to love mercy, and to walk humbly with your God?" (Micah 6:8).

Providence—Always *remember*...and never forget...the fact that our God "shall neither slumber nor sleep" (Psalm 121:4). No, He is *always* at work, in *every* detail of your life, working *all* things together for your good and for His purposes. Now, on to our next lesson where we'll learn more about God's providence.

Lesson 16

Turning the Heart of a King

*L*uck." "Fate." "Fluke." "Happenstance." "Coincidence." These terms litter the language of those who fail to accurately acknowledge the power and sovereign control of God over every detail of life.

When we ponder the events in the book of Esther, words like those above come to mind. However, when we learn that...at just the *right* time, King Ahasuerus couldn't sleep and...at just the *wrong* time Haman showed up in the court, we mustn't say, "What a coincidence!" We must instead say, "Wow! Behold the providence of God, the hand of God, the perfect timing of God, in these scenes!"

What is the providence of God? One definition explains that it's God making "all things, dark as well as light, crooked as well as straight, to co-operate to the furtherance and final completion of His high design."[24]

Before we move on in our narrative and discover what happens next, read these insightful words about the events of Esther, Chapter 6, the providence of God, and how God turns the heart of a king to further His high design for His people (Proverbs 21:1).

In this chapter we have a night interlude between the making of a gallows and the holding of a feast. In the economy of God, vast issues follow trivial things. A sleepless night is a matter transient and almost trivial. Yet...in the case of Ahasuerus, it was another of the ways along which God moved forward for the deliverance of His people.

To while away its hours, the king commanded his readers to read to him from the Records. Again, the unseen God, directing the mind of the king! When they obeyed, they found themselves reading an entry about a service Mordecai had rendered to the king. Again the unseen God, choosing the particular roll for their reading!

Then swiftly and suddenly things developed. Haman was waiting without, for the opportunity of asking that Mordecai be hanged. He entered, heard, and went forth to confer the highest dignities of the kingdom— upon Mordecai! Thus God works out His own high purposes, slowly as it seems oftentimes, but surely, and with unerring wisdom, until all things being done, the end is sudden, dramatic, complete....[25]

Truly, our God standeth within the shadows, keeping watch above His own! Let's see now which way he "turned the heart" of King Ahasuerus!

Esther 6:10-14

¹⁰ Then the king said to Haman, "Hurry, take the robe and the horse, as you have suggested, and do so for Mordecai the Jew who sits within the king's gate! Leave nothing undone of all that you have spoken."

¹¹ So Haman took the robe and the horse, arrayed Mordecai and led him on horseback through the city square, and proclaimed before him, "Thus shall it be done to the man whom the king delights to honor!"

¹² Afterward Mordecai went back to the king's gate. But Haman hurried to his house, mourning and with his head covered.

¹³ When Haman told his wife Zeresh and all his friends everything that had happened to him, his wise men and his wife Zeresh said to him, "If Mordecai, before whom you have begun to fall, is of Jewish descent, you will not prevail against him but will surely fall before him."

¹⁴ While they were still talking with him, the king's eunuchs came, and hastened to bring Haman to the banquet which Esther had prepared.

From the Heart of God's Word...

1. Read again Esther 6:6-9. After Haman's elaborate description of what he would do to honor another, what did King Ahasuerus command (Esther 6:10)?

How did the king refer to Mordecai (verse 10)?

Note the added instruction given to Haman (verse 10).

What did Haman do (verse 11)?

And what did Haman do afterward (verse 12)?

2. At a second gathering of family and friends, Haman explained what had happened to him regarding Mordecai. What did his listeners conclude (verse 13)?

3. Furthermore, what occurred while this discussion was taking place (verse 14)?

From Your Heart...

• *Regarding Mordecai*—After a long delay, Mordecai received acknowledgment for his good deed and faithful service. What does Mordecai and his situation teach you about your service and faithfulness?

And what do these principles from Scripture teach you?

Psalm 37:7—

Isaiah 55:8-9—

• *Regarding Haman*—As you read verse 12, can you imagine how Haman must have felt? Now look who's mourning (compare verse 12 with Esther 4:1-3)! In your own words, what was it that the king asked Haman to do? And in what ways was Haman humiliated?

How did these principles from Scripture apply to Haman?

Psalm 34:15-16—

Proverbs 16:18—

Cultivating a Heart
of Beauty & Strength

As we try to understand the events of the book of Esther, we can speculate why the king couldn't sleep: Did he eat too much? Drink too much? Was he excitedly looking forward to the next banquet? Was he anxious about Esther's request? We may guess the reason, but we know that it was the providence of God.

And we can be amazed at Haman's presence at the very moment that King Ahasuerus was inquiring about who was in the court. But once again…it was the providence of God.

And we can wonder at the fact that Mordecai's goodness was overlooked for so long; then suddenly, because of the king's sleepless night, he is honored in a royal way. But, one more time, the unanswerable is answered in the providence of God.

And you, my friend? You can struggle to understand the details of your life, but better it is to understand that all that happens to you—good and bad, large and small, earth-shattering and insignificant—is directly related to the providence of God. He faithfully overrules, intermingles, and causes the particulars of our lives to cooperate with each other until He brings His will to pass.

It's like making a chocolate cake. Have you ever thought about the ingredients for such a delight? They include something bitter (chocolate), something tasteless (flour), something sweet (sugar), something raw (eggs), and something sour (buttermilk). Yet when mixed together and passed through something hot (the fire of the oven), they produce a lovely confection.

Dear one, as you live your life, and as your days bring forth a parade of various people, events, and circumstances that are in themselves bitter, tasteless, sweet, raw, sour, and fiery, look to the divine providence of God. Know that in God's hands, the ingredients of your life will always work out for your good and for His eternal purposes (Romans 8:28). Trust Him to produce something lovely.

Pleading for Her People

Esther 7:1-10

Planning. Praying. Preparing. Our beautiful Esther teaches us many strong lessons on how to accomplish something, whether it's gaining the approval of another, determining the words to say (or not to say!), setting the scene for a delightful evening, or fixing a scrumptious meal.

But in our lesson today, we see that after all of the *planning*, *praying*, and *preparing*, finally Esther takes the plunge and *proceeds* toward her purpose of *pleading* for her people, the Jews. It's time...and everyone knows it. King Ahasuerus has waited and is properly expectant and curious. And Haman, too, has arrived, with some sense of foreboding birthed by the events of the day. Yes, it's time. So, let's see how it happens. Let's see how all of Esther's strength and beauty of character come into focus as she opens the door to welcome her visitors (and us) to a second spread.

Esther 7:1-10

¹ So the king and Haman went to dine with Queen Esther.

² And on the second day, at the banquet of wine, the king again said to Esther, "What is your petition, Queen Esther? It shall be granted you. And what is your request, up to half my kingdom? It shall be done!"

³ Then Queen Esther answered and said, "If I have found favor in your sight, O king, and if it pleases the king, let my life be given me at my petition, and my people at my request.

⁴ "For we have been sold, my people and I, to be destroyed, to be killed, and to be annihilated. Had we been sold as male and female slaves, I would have held my tongue, although the enemy could never compensate for the king's loss."

⁵ So King Ahasuerus answered and said to Queen Esther, "Who is he, and where is he, who would dare presume in his heart to do such a thing?"

⁶ And Esther said, "The adversary and enemy is this wicked Haman!" So Haman was terrified before the king and queen....

⁹ Now Harbonah, one of the eunuchs, said to the king, "Look! The gallows, fifty cubits high, which Haman made for Mordecai, who spoke good on the king's behalf, is standing at the house of Haman." Then the king said, "Hang him on it!"

¹⁰ So they hanged Haman on the gallows that he had prepared for Mordecai. Then the king's wrath subsided.

From the Heart of God's Word...

1. As Chapter 7 opens, who was in attendance at this banquet (verse 1)?

   For the third time (see also Esther 5:3 and 6) what did King Ahasuerus ask of Esther (Esther 7:2)?

   Now, at last, what answer did Esther give (verse 3)?

   a.

   b.

   And what explanation did she provide (verse 4)?

   What was to be done to Esther and her people under the terms of the "sale" (verse 4)?

2. What was the king's next question (verse 5)?

   And what was Esther's answer (verse 6)?

   How did she describe him (verse 6)?

3. How did Haman respond to Esther's accusation (verse 6)?

4. The man Harbonah observed something and perhaps made a subtle suggestion. What was it (verse 9)?

   And how did he describe Mordecai (verse 9)?

5. How did the skilled writer of the book of Esther summarize the climax of the book thus far and the events of Chapter 7 (verse 10)?

From Your Heart...

- A lot has happened in these few verses. Yet we need to know how these events apply to our lives and hearts. So let's get to the "heart" of Chapter 7. First, describe the manner in which Esther, ever the sensitive diplomat, made her requests.

  What can you consciously do to nurture the beauty and strength of wise speech and timing that she models for us? List at least three actions that will help you, too, to plan, pray, and prepare for such qualities of greatness.

  How do you see these principles from the Bible lived out in this chapter?

  Psalm 9:15-16—

  Proverbs 16:23—

  Ecclesiastes 3:1,7—

Cultivating a Heart of Beauty & Strength

Esther is beautiful and grand, isn't she? She is an exquisite portrait of a woman after God's own heart. She was quiet when quietness was called for, and vocal when a voice needed to be heard. And she chose wisely what to say and the order of presentation. She was careful. She was patient. And she was courageous. Far from being a woman on a mission of revenge, Esther acted only when she had to, and for a grand cause—to plead the cause of God's people. And she *proceeded* only after *planning*, *praying*, and *preparing*.

But…standing behind Esther, His woman of beauty and strength, is God Himself. As Dr. Charles Swindoll observes in his book on the beautiful life of Esther and the "surprising" sovereignty of God,

*E*sther, our heroine, is a lovely model to follow. And her story is certainly one to remember. But the best focus of all? God Himself. How perfectly He works, how sovereignly He controls, and how remarkably He changes the face of things, once He moves in. A queen who was once passive is suddenly in charge. A king who was once duped is now informed. An enemy who was only moments away from exterminating a nation is now an object of scorn. And even those ghastly gallows, once built for a Jew named Mordecai, will soon pierce the body of a Gentile named Haman.[26]

Now, don't stop here! The book of Esther doesn't! There's more action to come! Read on!

esson 18

Looking Out for Others

$\mathcal{A}$s Dr. Swindoll pointed out on the previous page, a queen who was once passive has now gone into action! However, only the initial results are in. Haman, the enemy of the Jews, is dead...but what about the scheduled massacre of God's people?! It's still on the docket of official business. And although it's planned for the thirteenth day of the twelfth month (still about six months away), Esther must continue to press ahead on the Jews' behalf. Truly she *has* come to the palace for such a time as this (Esther 4:14)!

Many times the ability to take action separates dreamers from doers, wishers from achievers. One gentleman put it this way—"The successful person is the individual who forms the habit of doing what the failing person doesn't like to do."[27] Well, one more noble trait of dear Esther's beauty and strength comes front stage today. Yes, she's alive—and so is Mordecai. And Haman's dead. But Esther needs to finish her job. She needs to follow through. She needs to speak up again. She needs to appeal to her husband the king one more time.

Take note how she does it. Then take note in your heart of this excellent trait of not quitting until the job is done.

Esther 8:1-8

1 On that day King Ahasuerus gave Queen Esther the house of Haman, the enemy of the Jews. And Mordecai came before the king, for Esther had told how he was related to her.

2 So the king took off his signet ring, which he had taken from Haman, and gave it to Mordecai; and Esther appointed Mordecai over the house of Haman.

3 Now Esther spoke again to the king, fell down at his feet, and implored him with tears to counteract the evil plot of Haman the Agagite, and the scheme which he had devised against the Jews....

5 and said, "If it pleases the king, and if I have found favor in his sight and the thing seems right to the king and I am pleasing in his eyes, let it be written to revoke the letters devised by Haman, the son of Hammedatha the Agagite, which he wrote to annihilate the Jews who are in all the king's provinces.

7 Then King Ahasuerus said to Queen Esther and Mordecai the Jew...

8 "You yourselves write a decree for the Jews, as you please, in the king's name, and seal it with the king's signet ring; for a letter which is

> written in the king's name and sealed with the
> king's signet ring no one can revoke."

From the Heart of God's Word...

1. How did King Ahasuerus honor Esther (verse 1)?

   And how did he honor Mordecai (verse 2)?

   Why (verse 2)?

   And what do you learn about a similar situation in Genesis 41:42?

2. Verse 3 shows us Esther's next *action*, verse 5 gives us the actual words of her *request*, and verse 8 records King Ahasuerus's *response*. Note each:

   Action (verse 3)—

   Request (verse 5)—

   Response (verse 8)—

3. We've seen it before (see Esther 1:19), but what reminder did the king give to Queen Esther and Mordecai about the Medo-Persian law in verse 8?

   What were Esther and Mordecai to do (verse 8)?

From Your Heart...

• Haman had destined thousands of the Jewish people to death. Therefore, Esther's request went far beyond herself. Rather than allow the king to become sidetracked by her *personal* safety (Esther 7:3-10), Esther moved to boldly plead again for his mercy on behalf of her *people*. What do you learn about character from her daring second entreaty?

- Compare Esther's approach before the king here with that of Esther 5:2-4. What differences do you note?

How might the differences be explained?

What principles should you embrace from her behavior?

- As Jesus said, "Ask, and it will be given to you" (Matthew 7:7). What do you learn from this and other lessons in our Esther study about...

  ...asking God?

  ...asking a husband?

  ...asking the right person?

  ...asking in the right way?

  ...asking repeatedly?

  ...asking passionately?

  ...asking humbly?

Cultivating a Heart of Beauty & Strength

Beauty and strength...beautifully evidenced as Esther, the queen, looks out for the lives of others. What do you think of these words, my friend?

*W*hen a person has gone up in the world and has achieved a position of power and eminence, it requires strength and beauty of character for that person still to love and remember the simple people from whom he, or she, sprang. Humble girls have often married rich men and have forgotten their origin. They have, in fact, been ashamed of anything that might remind them of it.[28]

No. Not our Esther! As a woman of rock-solid character, Esther kept her pledge to speak up...even if it meant she perished! She faithfully followed the advice of her guardian Mordecai and persevered to the end. She fought the battle upstairs, at the top, as a beautiful insider, for her people. She prepared. She prayed and fasted. She planned. And she proceeded, pushing ever forward on her mission of looking out for others.

And you, dear one? Don't think that such honorable opportunities are not available to you! You don't have to be a queen to speak up when it's that suitable "time to speak" (Ecclesiastes 3:7). You don't have to marry a king to harbor a heart that cares. You don't have to belong to the upper class to be used by God on behalf of His people. No. Wherever you are, "in whatever state" or condition you're in, within the circle of influence God has divinely drawn around your life, your heart of love for God, for His purposes, and for His people can shine brilliantly as you serve God to the limit of your ability.

$\mathcal{L}$esson 19

Sending Glad Tidings

$\mathcal{S}$uffering is a malady that no man or woman desires...or eludes. Everyone knows the pain of loss and of affliction. Trouble is a reality of life, and I'm certainly no stranger to suffering! As a result of my own experience concerning my husband's near-activation by The U.S. Army Reserves during the Persian Gulf War, I think I know a *little* about how the Jews felt as they mourned and waited for the fateful day to arrive when they were scheduled to be executed. And I think I know, too, a *little* about how they gloried in the glad tidings sent out by Queen Esther's cousin Mordecai. But wait...I don't want to get ahead of you! So please, read first...*then* we'll celebrate the glad tidings.

Esther 8:9-17

⁹ So the king's scribes were called at that time, in the third month, which is the month of Sivan, on the twenty-third day; and it was written, according to all that Mordecai commanded, to the Jews, the satraps, the governors, and the princes of the provinces from India to Ethiopia, one hundred and twenty-seven provinces in all, to every province in its own script, to every people in their own language, and to the Jews in their own script and language.

¹⁰ And he wrote in the name of King Ahasuerus, sealed it with the king's signet ring, and sent letters by couriers on horseback, riding on royal horses bred from swift steeds.

¹¹ By these letters the king permitted the Jews who were in every city to gather together and protect their lives—to destroy, kill, and annihilate all the forces of any people or province that would assault them, both little children and women, and to plunder their possessions

¹² on one day in all the provinces of King Ahasuerus, on the thirteenth day of the twelfth month, which is the month of Adar.

¹³ ...so that the Jews would be ready on that day to avenge themselves on their enemies.

¹⁴ Then the couriers who rode on royal horses went out, hastened and pressed on by the king's command. And the decree was issued in Shushan the citadel.

¹⁵ ...and the city of Shushan rejoiced and was glad.

¹⁶ The Jews had light and gladness, joy and honor.

¹⁷ And in every province and city, wherever the king's command and decree came, the Jews had joy and gladness, a feast and a holiday....

From the Heart of God's Word...

1. After Esther accomplished for her people what only she could accomplish inside the palace and with her husband, the king, Mordecai now took the helm. Newly appointed to the position of prime minister, so to speak, he dictated a new edict. Compare the wording of his edict with that written by Haman in Esther 3:12-13. What added group was Mordecai's letter addressed to (Esther 8:9)?

   What permission was granted to the Jews (verses 11-12)?

   And what was the purpose (verse 13)?

   And on what specific day (verse 12)?

2. How was the edict sent out (verses 10 and 14)?

   And what happened in Shushan (verse 14)?

3. With the letters written and sent on their way, how did the people react to the edict (verse 15)?

   What was the mood of the people after *Haman's* edict was published in Esther 3:15?

   And now after *Mordecai's* edict (Esther 8:15)?

4. Compare, also, the response of the Jews after *Haman's* edict (Esther 4:3)...

   ...and after *Mordecai's* here in Esther 8:16.

From Your Heart...

• God—using Esther and Mordecai and King Ahasuerus— has turned the tables for the Jews! Words of hope were penned to all Jews in the 127 provinces between India and Ethiopia. And the good tidings were stated...

Succinctly—Ever so carefully, so that there would be absolutely no misunderstanding, Mordecai's message on behalf of the king was that the Jews were allowed to defend themselves and their families on the specific day a previous edict had targeted as their annihilation. And the good tidings were dispatched...

Swiftly—The fastest thoroughbred racehorses from the king's stables were sent with the good news. Imagine how they flew! And the dust clouds behind them as they streaked across the desert lands! In the absence of telephones, electronic mail, fax machines, Fed-Ex delivery trucks, and priority mail, the fastest form of communication was chosen, perhaps with hopes that these swift steeds would even overtake the messengers sent out with Haman's edict. (Albeit horses, Romans 10:15 does come to mind: "How beautiful are the feet of those...who bring glad tidings of good things!")

What evidences of God's good providence and great love for His people do you glimpse in this passage of Scripture?

• Note the emotions Mordecai's glad tidings evoked from the Jews during their days of darkness:

> Rejoicing and gladness

> "Light" (or well-being) and joy and honor (as human beings)

> A feast and a holiday

Scholars concur that Israel had now begun to experience one of the greatest deliverances of God since the Exodus.

You have glad tidings and good news to share with others—the message of the deliverance of God of sinners through His Son, Jesus Christ. The gospel of Jesus Christ has the power to turn weeping into shouts of joy (Psalm 30:5), to turn mourning into dancing and to put off the shrouds of sackcloth and gird others with gladness (Psalm 30:11). Are you holding on to "the good news," or are you sending out the glad tidings by passing it on? Whom do you need to share the "light" with this week?

- And a further note...about Esther. For 8 chapters of the Bible and 19 lessons in our study, you and I have been sifting through Esther's behavior and deeds, looking for the gems of her strength and beauty of character. We've carefully noticed her words...and lack of them, her decisions...and how and why she made them, her corps of counselors (Mordecai)...and how she looked to him, her relationship with her husband...and how she treated him. Noting that the people are literally dancing in the streets and shouting for joy and celebrating their right to live, what contribution did our strong and "beautiful" Esther make to such a scene?

Are you aware that you, too, dear beautiful sister in Christ, can make such a contribution as you cultivate godly character and put it to use for God's people and purposes?

Cultivating a Heart of Beauty & Strength

And now, just a quick closing—and a beautiful thought about "light." In writing about the book of Esther, Dr. Herbert Lockyer shared this meditation: "Esther is the rose window in the cathedral structure of the Old Testament. If the light it transmits be dim, it reveals exquisite tracery and symbolic design in the framework and colored panes."[29] Esther herself has also brought us much "light" through her exquisitely colored panes, hasn't she?

And God certainly brought "light" to the Jews as He shined the spotlight of His great love and watchful care upon His people through the written words of Mordecai. Like the popular cheering at ball games called a "wave," riotous, abundant, profuse joy broke forth and rippled across the land as the king's horses raced into village after village with glad tidings.

Have you expressed the "light" of your joy to God today? Have you celebrated His love for you today? Regardless of any dark suffering, you can always rejoice in the "light" of the Lord (Philippians 4:4)!

Fighting for Right

Esther 9:1-10

*A*lthough we've not actually had "an Esther sighting" in a few lessons, we are without a doubt reading about the results of her bold moves on behalf of her people, the Jews. Bold moves that called for bold beauty and bold strength! Although Esther herself is silent (probably silently tucked away in the king's palace), her powerful contribution to the good of the Jews S-H-O-U-T-S from the text!

In the meantime, time has been ticking along. Time has a way of passing, sometimes slowly and other times with disturbing speed. But God stands watch not only over His people and His purposes, but also over time. He is the God of the sands of the hourglass. In His sovereign attention to detail, God had allowed the Jews *just enough time* to mourn (so that they could look to Him in prayer and fasting, preparing their souls), *just enough time* to celebrate (so that they could spend valuable time praising Him for His goodness), and *just enough time* to prepare for battle (so that they could organize and strategize and band together and, with God Almighty's assistance, seize the day and the victory!).

Now, let's see what happened next...

Esther 9:1-10

1 Now in the twelfth month, that is, the month of Adar, on the thirteenth day, the time came for the king's command and his decree to be executed. On the day that the enemies of the Jews had hoped to overpower them, the opposite occurred, in that the Jews themselves overpowered those who hated them.

2 The Jews gathered together in their cities throughout all the provinces of King Ahasuerus to lay hands on those who sought their harm. And no one could withstand them, because fear of them fell upon all people.

3 And all the officials of the provinces, the satraps, the governors, and all those doing the king's work, helped the Jews, because the fear of Mordecai fell upon them.

4 For Mordecai was great in the king's palace, and his fame spread throughout all the provinces; for this man Mordecai became increasingly prominent.

5 Thus the Jews defeated all their enemies with the stroke of the sword, with slaughter and destruction, and did what they pleased with those who hated them.

⁶ And in Shushan the citadel the Jews killed and destroyed five hundred men.

¹⁰ ...but they did not lay a hand on the plunder.

From the Heart of God's Word...

1. At last the fateful day had arrived. Eleven months had passed since the evil Haman supervised the casting of the lot (or the rolling of the dice). That's one full year and one month. We can only imagine how slowly (and terribly!) those dreadful days dragged by! But the day finally came—sometime in either February or March, 473 B.C. What two forces met on that day and why (verse 1)?

   How did the writer report the outcome (verse 1)?

   Verse 2 goes into a little more detail. How were the enemies of the Jews described?

   And why were they ineffective (verse 2)?

2. What new information do we learn in verse 3, and why?

   Describe Mordecai (verse 4).

3. How did the battle go, according to verse 5?

   How many attackers of the Jews were reported dead in Shushan (verse 6)?

4. How many times is the word "enemy" or "enemies" used in this passage, and where?

   And how many times is the word "hated" used in this passage, and where?

From Your Heart...

- *Purpose of the battle* (verses 1-2,5)—Over and over again, the writer of the book of Esther tells us the purpose of this bloody scene. Don't miss it! In your own words, what was the purpose? (You may want to read these verses again.)

  Think about your country, your family, your life. What are the "right" things you might go into a life-or-death battle for?

- *Person of Mordecai* (verses 3 and 4)—Mordecai is truly the man of the hour. His long list of character qualities is on parade as well. His time has come to take hold of the reins of the kingdom and guide it in God's direction. What traits have brought Mordecai to such a place of leadership?

  How does Mordecai's usefulness—even as he went un-noticed—encourage you in your roles in life?

  How can you be more faithful to those *you* serve?

- *Plunder of the goods* (verse 10)—Do the words regarding "the plunder" seem to you to be an afterthought? Well, they're not. In fact this information is so important that it will be repeated twice more in the lessons to come. What was the wording of the edict sent out in Esther 8:11?

  While the Jews had the rightful privilege of helping them-selves to the property and possessions of those who attacked them, they did not take advantage of it. No, their desire was singular—to defend themselves...not enrich themselves. They fought in self-defense for what was

right, and from pure motives. Their mission was to preserve the Jewish race...not to plunder the Persians. What
can we learn from their example in regards to greed?

* *Person of God*—Behold, the blessing of God! When it was
time for the Jews to defend themselves, "the opposite
occurred" (verse 1)—instead of being overpowered by
their enemies, the enemies of God's people were overpowered by them! As one version of the Bible declares, "It
was turned to the contrary" (KJV). *It?* Was *turned* to the
contrary? By whom? And how? The answers are obvious,
aren't they? The tables were turned by God in favor of
His beloved people, the apple of His eye. Instead of being
the victims, the Jews became the victors on that day...
thanks to the blessing of God!

Behold also, the hand of God! "Fear" fell upon all the
people, the non-Jews. There is obvious evidence here of
a supernatural influence. God was at work, behind the
scenes, in the shadows. His name may not appear in the
book of Esther, but His finger certainly does!

Can you think of some times or ways that God has
worked in your life through events that were unexpected
and seemed insignificant at the time? Or perhaps how you
came to be married to your mate? Or perhaps in the circumstances leading up to your becoming a Christian?
Share how God has directed you from the shadows.

Cultivating a Heart of Beauty & Strength

Seen...but not seen. This wonderful story, this important
little slice of history, is aglow with the reality of divine

providence! And, to the eye of faith and the attentive observer, "all history is a burning bush aflame with the mysterious presence."[31]

Faith, dear one, is seeing the unseen. As the Scripture says, "we walk by faith, not by sight" (2 Corinthians 5:7); and also, "faith is the substance of things hoped for, the evidence of things not seen" (Hebrews 11:1). Well, my friend, we've just "seen" that which is "not seen"—the invisible hand of God hovering over and protecting His people.

And another amazing evidence of the presence and providence of God is the way that He silently but oh-so-steadily works in the lives of His people. For instance...

Esther surprisingly found favor with Hagai, with all who saw her, with the king (Esther 2:9-17), and, obviously, with God (for "when a man's ways please the Lord, He makes even his enemies to be at peace with him"—Proverbs 16:7).

Mordecai remarkably found favor with not only the Jews, but with the people of the city, with the people in all the provinces, and with the governmental officials (Esther 8:15; 9:2-3).

Behold, the Person of God, the blessing of God, the hand of God, the providence of God, and the presence of God! As one academic explains, God is evident in the "tiny miracles" of God's providence that direct your steps.[32] Don't forget to watch for His "tiny miracles" in your life!

And here's another thought to ponder:

"Tell me," said a philosopher, "where is God?"

"First tell me," said the other, "where He is not."[33]

*esson 21

Finishing Fully

ecently I was enjoying a visit with my daughter Courtney, a busy homemaker, wife, and mother of a three-month-old and an eighteen-month-old. As we sat down at that wonderful moment when miraculously both babies were down for a nap—at the same time!—and began chatting, I heard Courtney say something like, "Basically my days are made up of just trying to finish a very few things fully."

I couldn't believe my ears! Was it possible that something *I* had worked on so hard while my two daughters were growing up had sunk into their hearts? Finishing fully! Yes, I spent a good decade learning the discipline of finishing fully. In fact, it appeared on my daily "to-do" list probably every day for those ten years.

Finishing fully is a trait that will bring you—and others—surprising benefits and blessings...just as it did Esther.

Esther 9:11-15

[11] On that day the number of those who were killed in Shushan the citadel was brought to the king.

[12] And the king said to Queen Esther, "The Jews have killed and destroyed five hundred men in Shushan the citadel, and the ten sons of Haman. What have they done in the rest of the king's provinces? Now what is your petition? It shall be granted to you. Or what is your further request? It shall be done."

[13] Then Esther said, "If it pleases the king, let it be granted to the Jews who are in Shushan to do again tomorrow according to today's decree, and let Haman's ten sons be hanged on the gallows."

[14] So the king commanded this to be done; the decree was issued in Shushan, and they hanged Haman's ten sons.

[15] And the Jews who were in Shushan gathered together again on the fourteenth day of the month of Adar and killed three hundred men at Shushan; but they did not lay a hand on the plunder.

From the Heart of God's Word...

1. On the awful designated day of confrontation, how many enemies of the Jews were killed in Shushan alone, including the ten sons of Haman (verse 12)?

Who proposed a second petition (verse 12)?

2. And how did Esther reply (verse 13)?

   a.

   b.

   When was all of this to occur (verse 13)?

3. What was the result of Esther's requests (verse 15)?

   What information is repeated in verse 15?

From Your Heart...

- As I spent time reading the research and comments of numerous scholars about the scene these verses describe, many seemed to interpret verse 12 as though it were written with exclamation marks. For instance...

  > And the king said to Queen Esther, "The Jews have killed and destroyed five hundred men in Shushan [alone]*!!!*"

  > "What have they [or must they have] done in the rest of the king's provinces?*!!!*"

  One senses that the king thought it was unbelievable that so many had openly attacked the Jews! On his own volition, King Ahasuerus next asks Esther if she has any further requests. What strong character quality (or qualities) is obvious in Esther's reply? Please explain.

- Again, what startling fact is revealed about the situation in Shushan in verse 15? Do you think Esther was right or wrong to ask for a second day of confrontation? And why?

Would you have been so bold? Or would you have weakened in your mission? (Remember Mordecai's charge to Esther, "Who knows whether you have come to the kingdom for such a time as this?"—Esther 4:14.) What are the worthy purposes God has led you to "fight" for? And are you faithfully following through, finishing fully?

List three tasks you need to follow through on this week (or today!). Then put Esther's strong and beautiful quality of persistence to work.

1.

2.

3.

Cultivating a Heart of Beauty & Strength

How can we become a woman like Esther who finishes fully?

Oh, you and I may never be called upon to stand before *a king*...but we'll stand before *the King*! We'll probably never be the kingpin in a tactical movement to save God's people...but we may well be the kingpin in a tactical movement to dispense God's Word to the little ones He's blessed us with so that they might enter into salvation (2 Timothy 3:15). We'll probably never be called upon to live in a palace...but we are called upon to turn the place we live in into a "palace" for our dear family. On and on goes our list of challenges to daily faithfulness...where *we* are...doing what *we* are supposed to do. And dear one, as women after

God's own heart, we're to cultivate—in our present situation—a *devotion to duty*, a strong *definition of purpose*, and look to the Lord for His help in the *discipline of self*.

At another time, when I was reflecting on this issue of faithfulness and the practice of finishing fully, I wrote these thoughts about "The Marks of Faithfulness."

*W*hat does faithfulness do? What does faithfulness in action look like? Well, if you were watching a woman who is walking with God by His Spirit, you would note these marks:

- She follows through—on whatever she has to do.

- She comes through—no matter what.

- She delivers the goods—whether a message or a meal.

- She shows up—even early so others won't worry.

- She keeps her word—her *yes* means *yes* and her *no* means *no* (James 5:12).

- She keeps her commitments and appointments—you won't find her canceling.

- She successfully transacts business—carrying out any instructions given to her.

- She discharges her official duties in the church—and doesn't neglect worship.

- She is devoted to duty—just as Jesus was when He came to do His Father's will (John 4:34).[34]

Celebrating God's Goodness

Esther 9:16-19

$\mathscr{E}$cclesiastes is categorized as one of the "wisdom" books of the Bible (along with Job, Psalms, Proverbs, and Song of Solomon). And is it ever full of wisdom! I especially enjoy Chapter 3, which deals with God's appointed "times" and "seasons."

Well, today we come to the appropriate "time" for laughter and dancing! As verses 1 and 4 of Ecclesiastes 3 put it, "To everything there is a season, a time for every purpose under heaven…

> A time to weep, And a time to laugh;
> A time to mourn, And a time to dance."

Much of the book of Esther has been about weeping and mourning (especially Esther 4:1-8). Both were fitting as the Jews faced annihilation and massacre due to Haman's death

126

decree. Both were proper responses as God's people dressed in sackcloth and ashes, fell on their knees, and beseeched God through prayer and fasting.

But today, ah, today! Read as God delivers the Jews from their enemies…and they break forth in feasting and festivity! Join in their joy!

Esther 9:16-19

¹⁶ The remainder of the Jews in the king's provinces gathered together and protected their lives, had rest from their enemies, and killed seventy-five thousand of their enemies; but they did not lay a hand on the plunder.

¹⁷ This was on the thirteenth day of the month of Adar. And on the fourteenth day of the month they rested and made it a day of feasting and gladness.

¹⁸ But the Jews who were at Shushan assembled together on the thirteenth day, as well as on the fourteenth; and on the fifteenth of the month they rested, and made it a day of feasting and gladness.

¹⁹ Therefore the Jews of the villages who dwelt in the unwalled towns celebrated the fourteenth day of the month of Adar with gladness and feasting, as a holiday, and for sending presents to one another.

From the Heart of God's Word…

1. What occurred in the provinces outside of the capital city of Shushan (verse 16)?

2. Finally the death toll is in. How many attackers of the Jews died in King Ahasuerus's provinces outside of Shushan (verse 16)?

And what fact is once again stated about the conduct of the Jews (verse 16)?

3. What was the natural response of the Jews to their victory over their enemies (verse 17)?

How did they celebrate (verses 17 and 19)?

4. This passage of Scripture shows us two groups of Jews. What facts distinguish the two? (Note: Those "in the king's provinces" and those "of the villages" are the same.)

From Your Heart...

- There are three important notations we need to make from this scene. First, *natural emotion*—God's people burst into spontaneous, natural celebration when their ordeal was over! What do you think they were celebrating? (Make as long a list as you like!)

  Now, what reasons do *you* have to celebrate God's goodness? (Again, you can make as long a list as you like.)

- Next, *natural order of events*—This passage is a little hard for some to understand. Why the two different days of celebration, we may wonder? To answer that question, remember that in Shushan there was a second day that the Jews were allowed to defend themselves (Esther 9:13-15). Therefore, their victory celebration came a day later. However, out in the provinces, there was one day of battle... and then blessed festivity!

- And finally, those celebrating here give you and me a *natural recipe for rejoicing*. List the "ingredients" included in this recipe for celebrating God's goodness.

  What additional "ingredients" from your list can you now add to your own celebrations of God's goodness to you?

Cultivating a Heart of Beauty & Strength

As I write this lesson, Father's Day is just two days away. It was a real joy this week to pray and plan and gather up the items I believe will help me to express my appreciation to my husband and two sons-in-law, each one of them a wonderful father. Plus, I've planned a celebration here at our home for Sunday afternoon. There will be "rest" (it's the Lord's Day). There will be feasting. There will be prayers and expressions of thanksgiving. There will be gift-giving and great joy.

Think, too, of your Christmas celebrations—both in your home and in your heart! Most Christians enjoy communal feasting with family and friends. Gifts are exchanged. The poor are remembered and ministered to. Yes, we tend to overspend as our generous hearts swell to include more and more people. Our joy is contagious, spontaneous, as we work to make sure no one is overlooked.

Well, my friend, are you getting the picture of this 127-province-wide instant celebration of God's goodness? We can be sure the Jews' emotions ran deep because their lives had been at stake...and God had come to their rescue.

Isn't the same true for you and me, when we stop to remember God's rescue of our souls from sin and darkness? How He brought us up out of a horrible pit and the miry clay, and set our feet upon a rock and established our steps (Psalm 40:2)? How He called us out of darkness into His marvelous light (1 Peter 2:9)? How, as a favorite hymn praises, "I once was lost but now am found, was blind but now I see"?[35]

Why not stop now and celebrate God's goodness?

esson 23

Remembering to Remember

ave you ever left a set of instructions for your children or for a babysitter or for a guest staying in your home? There are some things we feel we must go over and over. First we *say* them over and over...and then we *write* the directions out, just in case. It's sort of a "don't-forget-to..." list.

Well, at first glance this passage from the book of Esther looks like one giant repeat. And it is in many ways. But the practice of writing out memos is a good way to help people remember *what* to do, along with *how* and *when* and *where* and *why* to do it. And that's exactly what Mordecai is doing in our lesson today. Let's find out the facts of this Memo from Mordecai, so to speak.

Esther 9:20-28

²⁰ And Mordecai wrote these things and sent letters to all the Jews who were in all the provinces of King Ahasuerus, both near and far,

²¹ to establish among them that they should celebrate yearly the fourteenth and fifteenth days of the month of Adar,

²² as the days on which the Jews had rest from their enemies, as the month which was turned from sorrow to joy for them, and from mourning to a holiday; that they should make them days of feasting and joy, of sending presents to one another and gifts to the poor.

²³ So the Jews accepted the custom which they had begun, as Mordecai had written to them....

²⁶ So they called these days Purim, after the name Pur. Therefore, because of all the words of this letter, what they had seen concerning this matter, and what had happened to them,

²⁷ the Jews established and imposed it upon themselves and their descendants and all who should join them, that without fail they should celebrate these two days every year, according to the written instructions and according to the prescribed time,

²⁸ that these days should be remembered and kept throughout every generation, every family, every province, and every city, that these days of Purim should not fail to be observed among the Jews, and that the memory of them should not perish among their descendants.

From the Heart of God's Word...

1. *Who?*—First of all, who wrote this information (verse 20)?

   And *who* were the letters sent to (verse 20)?

   Where?—Where did the recipients live (verse 20)?

   Why?—Why were the letters written (verse 21)?

   When?—When was the celebration to occur (verse 21)?

   What?—What needed to be remembered (verse 22)?

   And *how* were the Jews to celebrate (verse 22)?

   Also *what* was the result of the sending of the letters (verses 23,26-28)?

2. Next we have a rehearsal of history (verses 24-25). Why was the celebration called "Purim" (verse 26)?

3. And a final *why*—*why* were these days to be celebrated without fail (verse 28)?

From Your Heart...

- Can you think of a specific time in your life when God turned your sorrow into joy and your mourning into a holiday? How can or do you remember it in celebration?

- Take a look at another kind of celebration Jesus told us to remember to remember in 1 Corinthians 11:24-26.

  How faithfully do you "remember" the Lord's death?

Cultivating a Heart of Beauty & Strength

Remembering to remember. It's too bad that it takes being reminded for us to celebrate and re-celebrate the wonderful grace of our Lord in our life! I once asked some women to share a situation where God had intervened and changed their sorrow into celebration. Here are a few of their praises:

- The day the doctor told me I would not need serious and life-changing surgery.

- The day God removed me from a very difficult [dating] relationship.

- The day I, a woman who can never get pregnant, held my best friend's first-born baby in my arms and was sincerely happy for her.

- The day my unsaved husband came to know and love the Lord Jesus Christ as his Savior!

- The day I became a Christian. I always celebrate it with a special "date" with God, a time of reflection and quiet time at the beach.

- The day I finally got a house on my own after my divorce, when many friends who had supported me through the hard times gathered to celebrate and help me move in.

Now, can you add your day to remember to this list written by other women after God's own heart? Remembering to remember builds beauty and strength of character. So don't forget to humbly and faithfully recall God's goodness and grace to you.

Sending Out the Word

Esther 9:29-32

You're probably acquainted with a time-management principle that advises us to write all special events on a 12-month calendar at the beginning of each new year. Why is this activity so useful? Because doing so ensures that we remember important occasions with each passing year.

Well, my friend, this practice of noting meaningful dates was already in operation 2,400 years ago. Queen Esther and her cousin Mordecai did something similar when they established a way of remembering how God had once again delivered the Jews from peril.

As you already know from our study of the book of Esther, the times had been dark as an edict was sent out by King Ahasuerus stating that all Jews could be murdered.

Imagine the heartache! The fear! The dread! It seemed that God's people could only wait for their doom.

And then picture the scene as the Jews were allowed by God to overpower their enemies! Imagine the joy! The jubilation! The sweet taste of victory! The relief!

To make sure the Jews then and in generations to come would never, *never* forget God's merciful act of salvation, Queen Esther sent out yet another decree to her people. Read these few additional details.

Esther 9:29-32

29 Then Queen Esther, the daughter of Abihail, with Mordecai the Jew, wrote with full authority to confirm this second letter about Purim.

30 And Mordecai sent letters to all the Jews, to the one hundred and twenty-seven provinces of the kingdom of Ahasuerus, with words of peace and truth,

31 to confirm these days of Purim at their appointed time, as Mordecai the Jew and Queen Esther had prescribed for them, and as they had decreed for themselves and their descendants concerning matters of their fasting and lamenting.

32 So the decree of Esther confirmed these matters of Purim, and it was written in the book.

From the Heart of God's Word...

1. First of all, please note that this is not the letter written in Esther 9:20. Instead it is a new letter...with a few new added ingredients. Who was listed first and what was said of her (verse 29)?

And how is the letter referred to in verse 32?

Who was listed first in the previous letter (Esther 9:20)?

2. We read twice here (verses 29 and 31) why this letter was sent out to all the Jews. What was that reason?

3. Compare the two directives (Esther 9:20-22 and 9:30-32). What is added to this second decree (verse 31)?

(Just a note: The book of Esther is still, to this day, read every year when the Jews faithfully celebrate the Feast of Purim. Obviously Esther's decree was taken seriously. It worked, fulfilling its purpose of reminding the Jews to remember their deliverance.)

Look again at Esther 4:15-17. Why might Esther and Mordecai make these practices a national custom?

4. What other "words" of encouragement were sent along with the second letter (verse 30)?

From Your Heart...

It's fairly easy to summarize this section from the book of Esther—it tells us that another letter was sent to the Jews throughout the Persian Empire by Esther, the queen, and Mordecai, repeating the prior instruction for the feast of Purim and adding fasting and lamenting (or crying out in distress) to the prescribed activities.

But for our purposes in this section on the commitment of God's word to our hearts, I want us to consider an overview of Esther's life and beauty of strength. First, read through these exciting facts about our beautiful Esther and then we'll walk through a set of thoughts for personal application.

Esther's strengths and accomplishments:

- Her beauty and character won the heart of Persia's king.
- She combined courage with careful planning.
- She was open to advice and willing to act.
- She was more concerned for others than for her own security.

Lessons from Esther's life:

- Serving God often demands that we risk our own security.
- God has a purpose for the situations in which he places us.
- Courage, while often vital, does not replace careful planning.[36]

- Do you know the word *winsome*? It means causing joy or pleasure, to be pleasant, winning, and cheerful. Do these definitions, better yet, these character traits, describe you? Why or why not?

Courage and careful planning—both mark a woman of beauty and strength. Do you measure up?

Hearing and acting on the advice of others—How do these twin evidences of wisdom depict your conduct?

A deep concern for others—Setting aside self is perhaps the noblest trait of all! Is this true of you?

Where has God placed you today? What is your "situation"? Do you remind yourself frequently that He has a grand purpose for you in exactly that place? *His* place? There's strength in that knowledge.

• Now think. Really think! Think of Esther's many beautiful qualities and strong characteristics. Our lessons have been packed with her admirable traits. The text in the box on the previous page spotlights several for you to admire. Plus I've shared some along the way.

But give some thought to this woman and exactly what it was that made her strong and beautiful. I don't want you to come to the end of our wonderful study of ten years in the life of such a wonderful woman and leave it with your own life and heart untouched, unchanged, unmoved. The purpose of studying the Bible is application. So think. Make your own list of Esther's many strong virtues. And then select at least three that you will seriously seek to nurture in the days to come.

1.

2.

3.

Cultivating a Heart of Beauty & Strength

It's been good to look upon Esther's beauty and strength again, hasn't it? She's been off the scene for a while. But in today's lesson, she bursts upon the page once again, "Queen" Esther writing with full authority to her people.

And, as we are beginning to draw the curtain on our study of this woman after God's own heart, I thought it was a good time to *remember* some of our Esther's loveliness and courage and *put into practice* what God has taught us in our study of His Word. Prayerfully list three principles or lessons you've learned from your study of the book of Esther that you desire to consciously apply, areas where you need change, areas where you wish to measure up more closely to God's beautiful standard.

1.

2.

3.

And now, as you faithfully work on applying these truths to your life, may our God pour out His abundant grace upon you and bless your efforts and transform you. May you know *His* beauty and *His* strength in your life. Amen.

Reflecting on Esther's Beauty & Strength

God, the unseen, unnamed Presence in the book of Esther, is also the author of this book detailing the deliverance of His people. And as the author, He chooses to end this book (and to close the historical section of the Bible) with a tribute to Esther's cousin Mordecai. After we hear God's commendations of Mordecai, we'll look one last time at the book of Esther and at Esther herself.

Now, behold the strength....of Mordecai!

Esther 10:1-3

[1] And King Ahasuerus imposed tribute on the land and on the islands of the sea.

2 Now all the acts of his power and his might, and the account of the greatness of Mordecai, to which the king advanced him, are they not written in the book of the chronicles of the kings of Media and Persia?

3 For Mordecai the Jew was second to King Aha-suerus, and was great among the Jews and well received by the multitude of his brethren, seeking the good of his people and speaking peace to all his kindred.

From the Heart of God's Word...

1. Describe Mordecai's position before the king (verse 3).

2. Describe the outstanding notations about Mordecai, his leadership, and his character (verses 2 and 3).

3. How was Mordecai looked upon by...

    the king (verse 2)—

    the Jews (verse 3)—

4. What were Mordecai's leadership objectives...

    for his people (verse 3)—

    for his countrymen (verse 3)—

From Your Heart...

- For our purposes, this study has centered on Esther, but it's impossible to walk away from this passage about her cousin Mordecai without taking notice of his character qualities. Which do you desire to be true of you, and why?

- How can you—like Mordecai—make a positive influence today on those around you? Spouse? Children? Family (even *your* cousins)? Friends? Neighbors? Your country?

Now, what's keeping you from doing so?

- For our final exercise, please enjoy this ten-letter acrostic outlining the ten chapters of the book of Esther.

> **P** ersian decree against Vashti
> **U** ncle [or cousin] Mordecai saves king
> **R** evenge plotted by Haman
> **I** ntercession made to Esther
> **M** aking dinner for Ahasuerus
> **F** avor shown to Mordecai
> **E** sther requests her life
> **A** hasuerus gives Mordecai promotion
> **S** ons of Haman hanged
> **T** estimony to Mordecai's greatness[37]

Now try *your* hand at an acrostic! Spell out the word Esther with some of the many qualities of beauty and strength you've witnessed in Esther's life.

E

S

T

H

E

R

Now...be sure to put these traits to work in your life! Then you, too, will bless others...just as Esther, God's woman of beauty and strength, did.

Cultivating a Heart of Beauty & Strength

It's been rich, hasn't it? I know we discussed earlier the fact that we as believers in Christ walk by faith and not by sight (2 Corinthians 5:7). And I hope it's wonderfully obvious by now that God, although unseen and unnamed, is "seen" watching over His people in every word and every detail throughout the book of Esther. And "though the name of God be not in it, the finger of God is, directing many minute events for the bringing about of His people's deliverance."[38]

So, dear one, we end our study of true beauty and strength with *God,* our magnificent and marvelous God. May you as a woman after God's own heart remember to remember these final words and apply them to your heart and life situation, no matter where God has placed you, and no matter how difficult your place is or seems to be:

In the book of Esther, we clearly see God at work in the lives of individuals and in the affairs of a nation. Even when it looks as if the world is in the hands of evil men, God is still in control, protecting those who are his. Although we may not understand everything happening around us, we must trust in God's protection and retain our integrity by doing what we know is right. Esther, who risked her life appearing before the king, became a heroine. Mordecai, who was on "death row" (so to speak), rose to become the Prime Minister of the nation. No matter how hopeless our condition, or how much we would like to give up, we need not despair. God is in control of our world.[39]

And now, dear woman after God's own heart, may our God make His beautiful grace to shine upon you and give you strength.

A Tribute

As I studied and digested material on the book of Esther, and worked on this study about becoming a woman of beauty and strength, I had to stretch my mind and my imagination to come to know Esther in her far-away setting long, long ago. *How old was she...really? What was her life in the palace like?*

How I thank God that in the midst of my writing I came to hear of a woman who fleshed out the exquisite qualities found throughout the book of Esther. She was young—barely 22 years old. Yet, in her brief life, her character had grown until its godly beauty reached out and touched forever the lives of those within the fragrance of her life. Her name is Natalie Christine Dyck. (I am purposefully using the present tense because our knowledge and memories of her live on and will always affect us deeply).

Just a few weeks after she graduated from The Master's College in Newhall, California, dear Natalie headed for Tanzania, Africa, where she was to spend the summer using her new degree in education to teach African children the English language and to share about God's love for them. And then, in the sovereign purposes and providence of the "true God who is all knowing, omnipresent, powerful, and in every way perfect" (these are words shared from Natalie's personal journal), on her way to minister alongside her missionary aunt and uncle, Natalie, along with 13 other people, died in a bus accident.

Natalie Dyck was truly a woman of deep inner beauty and strength. It was out of that lovely beauty and powerful faith that Natalie wrote these words: "The greatest joy in my life is to serve my Savior. Everything that I do, say, and think each day needs to be a reflection of the God that I serve. A quote that I have applied personally to my life is, 'My greatest joy in life is to bring a smile to my Savior's face.'"

I wanted you to know about this young woman, Natalie Dyck, this present-day Esther, whose character so abounded with the beauty of the Lord. May her life touch yours, dear one, as it has deeply touched mine through the testimony of so many who knew her well. These truths about *reputation* versus *character* that follow on the next page were printed on the program for Natalie's memorial service. May they point you to the value of being a woman of beauty and strength like Natalie, and to the priceless worth of hard-won godly character.

The circumstances amid which you live determine your reputation;
The truth you believe determines your character.

Reputation is what you are supposed to be;
Character is what you are.

Reputation is the photograph;
Character is the face.

Reputation comes over one from without;
Character grows from within.

Reputation is what you have when you come into a new community;
Character is what you have when you go away.

Your reputation is learned in an hour;
Your character does not come to light for a year.

Reputation is made in a moment;
Character is built in a lifetime.

Reputation grows like a mushroom;
Character grows like an oak.

A single newspaper report gives you your reputation;
A life of toil gives you your character.

Reputation makes you rich or makes you poor;
Character makes you happy or makes you miserable.

Reputation is what men say about you on your tombstone;
Character is what angels say about you before the throne of God.

—Author unknown

Notes

1. Herbert Lockyer, *All the Books and Chapters of the Bible* (Grand Rapids, MI: Zondervan Publishing House, 1978), p.108.

2. Neil S. Wilson, ed., *The Handbook of Life Application* (Wheaton, IL: Tyndale House Publishers, Inc., 1992), p. 648.

3. Joyce G. Baldwin, *Esther* (Downers Grove, IL: InterVarsity Press, 1984), p. 55.

4. Elon Foster, *6000 Sermon Illustrations*, quoting Hare (Grand Rapids, MI: Baker Book House, 1992), p. 658.

5. Baldwin, *Esther,* p. 62.

6. Ibid., p. 61.

7. Charles R. Swindoll, *Esther—A Woman of Strength and Dignity* (Nashville: Word Publishing, 1997), p. 30.

8. Eleanor Doan, *The Speaker's Sourcebook* (Grand Rapids, MI: Zondervan Publishing House, 1977), p. 210.

9. Merrill F. Unger, *Unger's Bible Dictionary* (Chicago: Moody Press, 1972), p. 897.

10. Joni Eareckson Tada, *Diamonds in the Dust* (Grand Rapids, MI: Zondervan Publishing House, 1993).

11. "Joni's Story," Joni and Friends, P.O. Box 3333, Agoura Hills, CA, 91301.

12. Elizabeth George, *Loving God with All Your Mind* (Eugene, OR: Harvest House Publishers, 1994), p. 183.

13. C. C. Carlson, *Corrie ten Boom: Her Life, Her Faith* (Old Tappan, NJ: F. H. Revell Co., 1983), p. 83.

14. *Life Application Bible Commentary—1 & 2 Timothy & Titus* (Wheaton, IL: Tyndale House Publishers, Inc., 1993), p. 49.

15. Karen H. Jobes, *The NIV Application Commentary—Esther* (Grand Rapids, MI: Zondervan Publishing House, 1999), p. 110.

16. Roy B. Zuck, *The Speaker's Quote Book* (Grand Rapids, MI: Kregel Publications, 1997), p. 26.

17. G. Campbell Morgan, *Life Applications from Every Chapter of the Bible* (Grand Rapids, MI: Fleming H. Revell, 1994), p. 137.

18. Zuck, *The Speaker's Quote Book*, p. 9.

19. Wilson, *The Handbook of Life Application*, p. 269.

20. Jeanette Lockerbie, *Esther: Queen at the Crossroads* (Chicago: Moody Press, 1975).

21. *Life Application Bible* (Wheaton, IL: Tyndale House Publishers, 1988), p. 769.

22. Howard F. Vos, *Bible Study Commentary—Ezra, Nehemiah, and Esther* (Grand Rapids, MI: Zondervan Publishing House, 1987), p. 165.

23. Albert M. Wells, Jr., *Inspiring Quotations—Contemporary & Classical* (Nashville: Thomas Nelson Publishers, 1988), p. 25.

24. Robert Jamieson, A. R. Fausset, and David Brown, *Commentary on the Whole Bible* (Grand Rapids, MI: Zondervan Publishing House, 1973), p. 1163.

25. Morgan, *Life Applications from Every Chapter of the Bible*, p. 138.

26. Swindoll, *Esther—A Woman of Strength and Dignity*, p. 136.

27. Wells, *Inspiring Quotations—Contemporary & Classical*, quoting Donald Riggs, p. 191.

28. Herbert Lockyer, *The Women of the Bible*, quoting H. V. Morton (Grand Rapids, MI: Zondervan Publishing House, 1975), p. 53.

29. Lockyer, *All the Books and Chapters of the Bible*, p. 109.

30. Vos, *Bible Study Commentary—Ezra, Nehemiah, and Esther*, pp. 180-81.

31. Lockyer, *All the Books and Chapters of the Bible*, p. 108.

32. Jobes, *The NIV Application Commentary—Esther*, p. 160.

33. Doan, *The Speaker's Sourcebook*, p. 113.

34. Elizabeth George, *A Woman's Walk with God* (Eugene, OR: Harvest House Publishers, 2000), p. 151.

35. "Amazing Grace," by John Newton.

36. *Life Application Bible*, p. 771.

37. Barry Huddleston, *The Acrostic Bible* (Portland, OR: Walk Thru the Bible Press, Inc., 1978).

38. Matthew Henry, *Commentary on the Whole Bible—Volume 2* (Peabody, MA: Hendrickson Publishers, 1996), p. 866.

39. *Life Application Bible*, p. 776.

Bibliography

Baldwin, Joyce G. *Esther*. Downers Grove, IL: InterVarsity Press, 1984.

Jamieson, Robert, A.R. Fausset, and David Brown. *Commentary on the Whole Bible*. Grand Rapids, MI: Zondervan Publishing House, 1973.

Jobes, Karen H. *The NIV Application Commentary: Esther*. Grand Rapids, MI: Zondervan Publishing House, 1999.

Life Application Bible. Wheaton, IL: Tyndale House Publishers, 1988.

Lockyer, Herbert. *All the Books and Chapters of the Bible*. Grand Rapids, MI: Zondervan Publishing House, 1978.

MacArthur, John, Jr. *The MacArthur New Testament Commentary—James* Chicago: Moody Press, 1998.

Pfeiffer, Charles F. and Everett F. Harrison. *The Wycliffe Bible Commentary*. Chicago: Moody Press, 1973.

Swindoll, Charles R. *Esther: A Woman of Strength and Dignity*. Nashville: Word Publishing, 1997.

Vos, Howard F. *Bible Study Commentary—Ezra, Nehemiah, and Esther*. Grand Rapids, MI: Zondervan Publishing House, 1987.

Whitcomb, John C. *Esther: The Triumph of God's Sovereignty*. Chicago: Moody Press, 1979.

Personal Notes

About the Author

Elizabeth George is a bestselling author who has more than four million books in print. She is a popular speaker at Christian women's events. Her passion is to teach the Bible in a way that changes women's lives. For information about Elizabeth's speaking ministry, to sign up for her mailings, or to purchase her books visit her website:

www.ElizabethGeorge.com

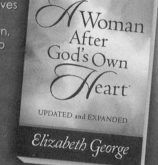

A Woman After God's Own Heart® Study Series

Bible Studies for Busy Women

God wrote the Bible to change hearts and lives. Every study in this series is written with that in mind—and is especially focused on helping Christian women know how God desires for them to live."

—Elizabeth George

Sharing wisdom gleaned from more than 20 years as a women's Bible study teacher, Elizabeth has prepared insightful lessons that can be completed in 15 to 20 minutes per day. Each lesson includes thought-provoking questions, insights, Bible-study tips, instructions for leading a discussion group, and a "heart response" section to make the Bible passage more personal.

Living with Passion and Purpose — LUKE — Elizabeth George
978-0-7369-0816-0

Becoming a Woman of Beauty & Strength — ESTHER — Elizabeth George
978-0-7369-0489-6

Putting On a Gentle & Quiet Spirit — 1 PETER — Elizabeth George
978-0-7369-0290-8

Discovering the Treasures of a Godly Woman — PROVERBS 31 — Elizabeth George
978-0-7369-0818-4

Nurturing a Heart of Humility — CHARACTER STUDY: MARY — Elizabeth George
978-0-7369-0300-4

Walking in God's Promises — SARAH — Elizabeth George
978-0-7369-0301-1

Experiencing God's Peace — PHILIPPIANS — Elizabeth George
978-0-7369-0289-2

Pursuing Godliness — 1 TIMOTHY — Elizabeth George
978-0-7369-0665-4

Cultivating a Life of Character — JUDGES/RUTH — Elizabeth George
978-0-7369-0498-8

Growing in Wisdom & Faith — JAMES — Elizabeth George
978-0-7369-0490-2

HARVEST HOUSE PUBLISHERS
EUGENE, OREGON 97402
www.harvesthousepublishers.com

Books by Elizabeth George

- Beautiful in God's Eyes
- Finding God's Path Through Your Trials
- Life Management for Busy Women
- Loving God with All Your Mind
- A Mom After God's Own Heart
- Powerful Promises for Every Woman
- The Remarkable Women of the Bible
- Small Changes for a Better Life
- A Wife After God's Own Heart
- A Woman After God's Own Heart®
- A Woman After God's Own Heart®
  Deluxe Edition
- A Woman After God's Own Heart®—A
  Daily Devotional
- A Woman After God's Own Heart®
  Collection
- A Woman's Call to Prayer
- A Woman's High Calling
- A Woman's Walk with God
- A Young Woman After God's
  Own Heart
- A Young Woman After God's
  Own Heart—A Devotional
- A Young Woman's Call to Prayer
- A Young Woman's Walk with God
- Walking with the Women of the Bible

Children's Books

- God's Wisdom for Little Girls
- A Little Girl After God's Own Heart

Study Guides

- Beautiful in God's Eyes
  Growth & Study Guide
- Finding God's Path Through Your Trials
  Growth & Study Guide
- Life Management for Busy Women
  Growth & Study Guide
- Loving God with All Your Mind
  Growth & Study Guide
- A Mom After God's Own Heart
  Growth & Study Guide
- The Remarkable Women of the Bible
  Growth & Study Guide
- Small Changes for a Better Life
  Growth & Study Guide
- A Wife After God's Own Heart
  Growth & Study Guide
- A Woman After God's Own Heart®
  Growth & Study Guide
- A Woman's Call to Prayer
  Growth & Study Guide
- A Woman's High Calling
  Growth & Study Guide
- A Woman's Walk with God
  Growth & Study Guide

Books by Jim & Elizabeth George

- God Loves His Precious Children
- God's Wisdom for Little Boys
- A Little Boy After God's Own Heart

Books by Jim George

- The Bare Bones Bible™ Handbook
- The Bare Bones Bible™ Bios
- A Husband After God's Own Heart
- A Man After God's Own Heart
- The Remarkable Prayers of the Bible
- The Remarkable Prayers of the Bible
  Growth & Study Guide
- A Young Man After God's Own Heart